# Burma's Spring

*Real Lives in Turbulent Times*

T0158237

# Burma's Spring

## Real Lives in Turbulent Times

Rosalind Russell

RIVER

BOOKS

First published and distributed in 2015 by
River Books
396 Maharaj Road, Tatien, Bangkok 10200
Tel. 66 2 622-1900, 224-6686
Fax. 66 2 225-3861
E-mail: order@riverbooksbk.com
www.riverbooksbk.com

Editor: Narisa Chakrabongse
Production supervision: Paisarn Piemmettawat
Design: Ruetairat Nanta

ISBN 978 616 7339 55 9

Printed and bound in Thailand
by Bangkok Printing Co., Ltd.

For Dan

# Contents

# A note on names

The use of names in Burma has been politically contentious over the years. In 1989 the governing junta changed the country's name to Myanmar, a move opposed by democracy advocates who stuck with Burma. Today, foreign governments are divided over which name to use – Britain and the United States still officially refer to Burma, but many countries have shifted to the use of Myanmar.

As 'Burma' and 'Rangoon' may be more familiar to readers outside the country than 'Myanmar' and 'Yangon', I have mostly used the old colonial names, although not entirely consistently.

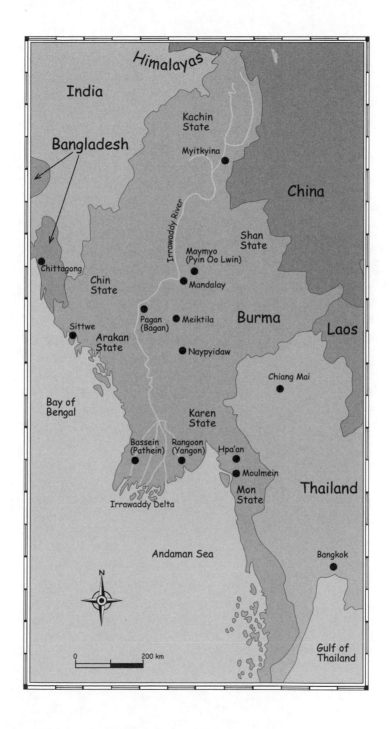

# The Saffron Revolution

Standing up, with the phone to my ear, I was stealing sideways glances at my reflection in the window, trying to work out how pregnant I really looked. Outside, tropical darkness had fallen on another Bangkok day, and the lights inside meant the floor-to-ceiling windows reflected back the scene in our living room. My nearly two-year-old daughter, bathed and warm-skinned, was in her pyjamas, engrossed in a self-invented game. I was on the phone, pacing, talking to editors in Singapore and London, trying to sort out a 'string' to go to Burma. I had a visa, I even had an air ticket, but I needed to feel that someone was actually *sending* me, that the story was big and important enough to justify missing my daughter's birthday the following day and a hospital appointment to check the progress of my pregnancy, now in its sixth month.

Of course, I questioned whether it was a good idea at all, especially when the Reuters editor in Singapore said I couldn't report for them because I was pregnant and uninsured. But these are peaceful demonstrations, I thought, I'll be fine. I kept dialling the numbers. *The Times* were sending their staff correspondent, he had just picked up his visa; the *Guardian*, no, but the *Independent*, yes, and Sky News too. I was going. The next morning, I took my daughter to her nursery with a supermarket-bought chocolate cake and two birthday candles, gave her a squeeze and jumped in a cab to the airport.

It was September 2007, nearing the end of the monsoon season. Burma, geographically right next door to Thailand but in every other sense a world away, was locked under military rule. The Asian economic miracle had swept over its skies leaving it untouched by late twentieth-century development. In August, the ruling junta, the intimidatingly named State Peace and Development Council, had removed subsidies on energy and fuel, causing a spike in food and transport costs and instant hardship for Burmese people already living on the margins of survival. Overnight, workers found they could not afford the bus fare into town; families did not have enough to buy rice and cooking oil. The first anti-government protests in a decade broke out in towns and cities across the country and were dealt with by the military with its usual method of detentions and beatings. Defiant, the people marched on, and by early September the country's Buddhist monks had joined them. Their numbers swelled, until rivers of cinnamon-robed monks flowed each day through the cities of Rangoon, Mandalay, Moulmein and Pakokku. They marched in bare feet or in their tattered black-velvet flip-flops. In nearly half a century of military rule there had been uprisings before, all put down with force. But the participation of the monks, revered and untouchable in Burmese society, created a challenging new predicament for the generals. They couldn't shoot, surely? Could Burma be on the brink of change?

On Thursday 27 September, when the monks had been marching for two weeks, I landed at Rangoon's international terminal and turned my watch back half an hour to Burma's idiosyncratic time zone. There were other journalists on the plane, I was sure of that, their noses in their Lonely Planet guidebooks, their cameras a little too highly specced to belong to a backpacker. Foreign reporters were banned from Burma, and we had filled out our landing cards with what seemed to be likely occupations – teacher, student, aid worker. We stood in the immigration queue, affecting nonchalance, tilting our heads up as if fascinated by the ceiling, before surreptitiously casting looks left and right. We shuffled wordlessly up the passport queue. My turn came and I stepped up to the counter to meet my first Burmese government official, a young, apple-cheeked female immigration officer, her hair pulled back in a bun fixed with a pink net. Most of the passport staff were women, in a uniform of short-sleeved white shirts with epaulettes, black A-line skirts, black socks that reached halfway up the calf and black court shoes with a sensible, two-inch heel. I was already of the firm belief that this woman was a bad person, a lackey of an evil regime. But then I couldn't help but be disarmed by her sweet manner and what seemed to be unworldly curiosity, rather than suspicious scrutiny, in her examination of my passport. It was the first hint that things would not be as I expected in Burma; the same contradiction between perception and reality would strike many times during the years I would spend there.

Out into the heat of the taxi scrum, I took a deep breath of damp Rangoon air, its scent a fusion of diesel and cardamom. I negotiated a fare and we sped past groaning buses, vegetable carts, karaoke bars and noodle stalls to the first of four hotels I would stay in that week. My driver was quiet, and I was too paranoid to ask questions. I had read about the government's network of informants and my guard was up. Around me life seemed normal, but I was expectant, excited by what I was going to find, already taking mental notes for the story I would file at the end of the day. I checked in, deposited my bag in my room and made a phone call to a Canadian friend, the head of an international aid agency in Rangoon. Up to now, the marchers had gathered around the golden Shwedagon pagoda, the focus of protests since the days of British rule. But word had it that today protesters were heading downtown to Sule, the city's smaller temple, another traditional rallying point for students and monks.

I walked out of the air-conditioned lobby and the uniformed doorman clapped to call a taxi from the rank. It was another typical Rangoon cab, a battered Toyota saloon from the early 1980s with a bouncing back seat of broken springs and doors stripped down to the metal chassis. I asked to go downtown. The driver, whose seat had been replaced by a metal-framed deck chair upholstered with plastic straps and bolted down to the original moorings, was relaxed and chatty in his broken English. But as we turned the corner on to Bogyoke Aung San Street, in front of the famous Scott Market, we felt the atmosphere change with a thump. People were running towards us, fear and panic written on their faces. Drivers were screeching their cars round and speeding back on the wrong side of the street. My driver started to turn too, and, making an instinctive decision not to retreat, I thrust a crumpled banknote into his hand and jumped out into the confusion of the street.

Stallholders were hurriedly bundling away their vegetables, DVDs and rails of children's clothes. Metal shutters clattered down on shop fronts. Two boys, bare-footed postcard-sellers aged no more than nine or ten, ran up to me, still clutching their images of tourist scenes. 'Madam, it is dangerous for you!' My heart was drumming, I could taste the danger, but I hadn't yet worked out what it was. With no concern for their own safety, the boys began to lead me over a footbridge towards the towering Traders Hotel. We scurried down the steps and along the broken pavement. Rounding the corner to Rangoon's main avenue, with the gleaming Sule at the far end, we met a cloud of smoke. People were running towards us, and I could see the khaki uniforms of soldiers further down the street. A group of panicked youths sped past carrying a man in a bloodstained shirt, his face knotted in pain. They each held one of his limbs, and his wounded body bounced around as they scrambled towards the junction. The crackle of gunfire came then, the sound unmistakable. The boys ran off and I squeezed myself through the metal barricades that had been hastily erected around Traders, ignoring the pleas of the security guard who tried to stop me getting to the hotel door.

The manager, in a fitted white blouse and black pencil skirt, was in the doorway keeping guard, her eyes narrow, her hair scraped back in an immaculate chignon.

'Are you a guest?' she asked, her voice clipped and hostile.

'Yes, well no, but look, I'm pregnant, please, I need to come in.'

'Guests only,' she insisted.

'Please,' I begged.

'Well, you can come through but we will escort you out of the back door.'

'That doesn't help me,' I said.

'Guests only.'

'Well, can I book a room?'

'It's 150 dollars plus tax.' She looked triumphant.

'Fine,' I said.

At the front desk I asked for a room overlooking the street, not caring now if they suspected me to be a journalist. 'Any luggage?' said the receptionist. 'No.' In silence, the concierge took me up in the lift. He opened the door to my eighth-floor room and showed me the air conditioner, the minibar and the complimentary fruit basket. The window stretched across the width of the room. I had a grandstand view of the terror below.

Protesters were fleeing en masse from the pagoda and soldiers followed them, advancing in strict formation. From eight floors up, I could hear the rhythmic stamping of their boots on the hot tarmac. The demonstrators that day were not monks, but mostly young men in T-shirts and sarong-style Burmese *longyis*. I heard later that the junta had launched pre-dawn raids on Buddhist monasteries, leaving bloodstains on the floors after they beat up and dragged away hundreds of monks. In the monks' absence, the soldiers were free to start shooting. The young men on the streets looked terrified, but also filled with rage. They first ran from the advancing army, then stopped, hesitant. Some turned back towards the soldiers as if considering a final charge, then, defeated, picked up rocks and threw them frustratedly, pointlessly, at a traffic police shelter on the corner.

I left my room to go to a north-facing window at the end of the corridor. There were three of us there: with me were a bellboy who had abandoned his post, and a middle-aged Western man who I assumed to be another journalist. We watched an unmarked van crawl along in front of the hotel. A loudhailer mounted on top blared instructions. *'Clear the area or we will take extreme action!'* His eyes still fixed on the street, the bellboy became our translator. The protesters reached an intersection where they grouped together and began chanting, *'Give us freedom! Give us freedom!'* A strange, primal roar went up – a last show of defiance. Anxious to keep our cover, the other reporter and I made no attempt at introductions. From the window we could see that the protesters were trying to regroup at the railway station. More people were arriving, piling out of minibuses and trucks. Their unity made them stronger, but by then they knew that they were stepping into the line of fire. By the time of the curfew that night, state media reported a death toll of nine, including a Japanese news photographer who was shot dead by soldiers near the Sule pagoda. In fact, far more were killed; opposition groups later put the toll at 138. The shooting sprees were going on all over the city, away from the lenses of the international press.

*✷ ✿ ✿ ✿ ✿ ✿ ✷*

The next morning, when the rain had cleared, I met up with an Irish colleague from Reuters who had flown in from her base in the Philippines, also undercover. We greeted each other by the hotel reception desk, pretending to be tourists nonplussed by the goings-on outside. Against the advice of the concierge, we took a taxi, saying we wanted to do a little sightseeing around town. We drove out of the hotel and turned right up a deserted Anawrahta

Street. As we approached an intersection the driver slowed. We looked to the right, down 28th Street, to see a platoon of soldiers in dark green uniforms advancing towards us, rifles at the ready, their red neckerchiefs signalling that they were armed with live rounds. Our heads turned left to see around twenty protesters, some with bandanas tied around their faces, panicked and dispersing. The taxi driver sped on.

Around us, shops were shut and few city residents had ventured out. But the quiet on the streets was no indicator of peace. Throughout that day, there were bids by demonstrators to regroup all around Rangoon. The city now bristled with soldiers who swooped on each attempt at a gathering. Military policemen were stationed on every corner. Army trucks patrolled streets empty of cars and buses. We saw soldiers stop and search a group of young men walking around the city centre, ordering them to squat down while they checked their papers, a calculated humiliation.

I needed to talk to people, find out what they were thinking. After the taxi deposited us back at Traders, I went for a quick walk around the city centre. It seemed that no one would look at me. A bookseller stood in his shop doorway and watched the young soldiers stopping the passers-by.

'What's going on?' I asked him.

'In this country, we are all blind and deaf,' he said. 'People have learned to keep quiet.'

I went up to the glittering Shwedagon pagoda, thinking it would be a safe place from which to report. The gates were open, but Burma's most sacred Buddhist site was now a military encampment. The monks had vanished; replaced by rifle-toting soldiers, lounging, smoking, uniforms unbuttoned in the heat. Their bare feet were their only concession to their holy surroundings. Two women, volunteer cleaners, were sweeping the marble floor. Wordlessly, they swept the dried grasses of their brooms past the soldiers' feet, with angry sideways glances at the temple's new guardians. The city was seething.

By night the crackdown continued, morphing into a hidden campaign of physical punishment and psychological terror no less horrifying than the shooting on the streets. The revolution was being systematically crushed. Under the cover of curfew, soldiers raided monasteries, beating and arresting monks. The thuggish paramilitary group Swan Ar Shin (Masters of Force) helped to round up thousands despite the efforts of civilian vigilante groups armed only with rocks and sticks to protect the clergy by blocking monastery gates. Rumours spread that the Government Technical Institute, a leafy college in Rangoon's northern suburbs, had been converted into a prison camp for suspected dissidents. Civilian demonstrators were not exempt. Officers from the Military Intelligence Agency scrutinised their video footage and photos, and sought tip offs from their spies in the townships. Anyone who had taken part in the protests, and even those who had watched, applauded, or handed a cup of water to a marching monk, could expect a night-time knock at the door, to be hauled off to a cell.

My own fears grew that I would be uncovered as a reporter. It was no secret that Traders was crawling with journalists and, despite its comfort and reliable phone lines, it was not the place to stay. In the hotel bar at night, the drinkers – so obviously journalists in their photographers' vests and desert boots and no doubt bursting with stories of near arrest and bullets dodged – sat alone with their beers, dolefully scooping palmfuls of peanuts into their mouths. I checked out and moved into an anonymous hotel across the road, only to be told the next day it was a 'government place' and I moved again. The regime had cut off the Internet to stop news circulating inside and to the outside world. Mobile phone access was strictly controlled – there was no roaming signal in Burma, my own phone was useless and a local SIM card cost thousands of dollars. I did my two-ways to Sky News on the hotel telephone, and painstakingly dictated long stories to the *Independent*. Each day I was out in different parts of the city. I was too visible; I was taking too many risks. There were clicks and interference on the phone line, and several times it cut dead. My paranoia grew. A knock on my hotel room door made my stomach lurch. Just the lady from housekeeping. Receptionists, taxi drivers, the people in the hotel coffee shop all began to look like regime spies to me. I was convinced they knew what I was up to and were ready to report me. Looking back, I'm sure I was wrong. The Burmese people had wanted the uprising to succeed. But they were too afraid to say so.

# Introduction

On the wall of my great-aunt Angela's dark, heavily furnished sitting room in Edinburgh hung a silk tapestry depicting St George, styled as a classical Burmese warrior, spearing a mythical dragon. She had sewn it herself, beginning the task beneath a whirring ceiling fan in her home in Rangoon during the Second World War. Growing up, I was told the story of the tapestry many times by different family members. At the outbreak of the war, Angela and my great-uncle Douglas were a young married couple living in colonial Burma, members of a large Scottish expatriate community oiling the wheels of imperial enterprise. My great-uncle was a solicitor, with an office on what was then Phayre Street, a short stroll from Rangoon's port.

Their life, as I imagine it now, was doubtless very comfortable; home would have been a picturesque, whitewashed villa with a manicured lawn. They would have engaged a full retinue of staff, leaving Angela plenty of time for her consuming hobbies – needlepoint and bridge. At weekends they may have enjoyed the horse races or boating on the lake, and evening entertainment (both were keen whisky drinkers) would have centred around the European clubs, perhaps the Pegu or the Gymkhana. What's certain is that their Rangoon life would have been much brighter than the dreary existence they might have expected had they remained in Depression-era Scotland.

Their colonial idyll came to an abrupt end, however. The invasion of Japanese forces in early 1942 forced Angela and Douglas, along with tens of thousands of other European and Indian expatriates in Burma, to flee with just the clothes on their backs (or, in Aunt Angela's case, with the clothes on her back plus her unfinished, six-by-four-foot tapestry). As the Japanese advanced westwards towards Rangoon, she and her husband escaped north to Mandalay. From there, by bullock cart and on foot, they embarked on a five-hundred-mile trek through rainforest infested with leeches, across turbulent rivers and along treacherous mountain passes in a desperate attempt to reach safety in India.

More than four thousand people died in the exodus, succumbing to malaria, typhoid, starvation and exhaustion. But my uncle and aunt were among the fortunate ones. On 23 April 1942, colonial records show they crossed the border to India, and later registered as refugees in Calcutta. The survival of the young couple and the unfinished tapestry against such great odds became the stuff of family legend. Back home in Scotland, Angela completed the elaborate work, this time at the fireside, expertly repairing the damage the tapestry had sustained during a Japanese air raid on their retreating convoy. It was whispered that the shrapnel injuries she had suffered in the bombardment were the reason the couple remained childless, and Angela's tapestry was passed down to my sister, an heirloom affectionately regarded as a symbol of courage and resilience.

❧ ✿ ✿ ✿ ✿ ✿ ✿ ❧

Burma seeped into my consciousness from an early age, but only as a backdrop to the heroic wartime feats of my ageing relatives. I heard much more about the manner of their departure from Burma than the place they had left behind. They would have lived in the shadow of the magnificent Shwedagon pagoda, toured the thousand-year-old temples of Pagan, cooled off in the hill station of Maymyo, but this was never discussed. I had no clear image of Burma other than of somewhere dangerous and inhospitable. Backpacking in Thailand in the 1990s, a trek through the jungles of the Golden Triangle brought us a hillside away from the Burmese border. Looking west towards the sinking sun, I observed how the thick forest of Burma's Shan state rose and fell to the dimming horizon, but without particular curiosity. It was a closed country, we were told, and we asked few questions. Of course I had read about Aung San Suu Kyi, the graceful wife of an Oxford don, imprisoned in her Rangoon home for standing up to Burma's military leaders. But when I started my career as a journalist, my job took me in other directions: to the Reuters bureau in East Africa, then the Caucasus, Afghanistan and Iraq. It wasn't until early in 2004, back in London from Baghdad, that Burma flickered on my radar once more.

In a noisy Moroccan restaurant in Clapham, my husband Dan was introducing me to a Canadian couple he had met in Angola. Like Dan, Andrew and Kelly worked for international aid agencies, and had spent the previous decade criss-crossing Africa, with postings from Addis Ababa to Ouagadougou. Now they had a young daughter, were expecting their second child, and were about to leave on their next assignment.

'Myanmar,' said Kelly over the dishes of tagine, leaning in over her pregnant belly.

'Where?'

'MEE-AN-MA,' she enunciated.

Oh yes, I had heard of that. Myanmar was the name the military government had given Burma. I felt mildly alarmed. Was a pariah, army-ruled state really the right place to take a family? But Andrew and Kelly had been assured that the Rangoon (or Yangon as it was now known) was far safer than any of the African cities in which they had lived, and with few Western brands (sanctions had ensured that) and little modern development, it retained the leafy charm of bygone Asia. Rangoon, I would later discover, enchanted its small expatriate community of diplomats and aid workers who cheerfully sacrificed the conveniences of a working banking system and reliable Internet for the blessings of gentle Burmese hospitality. Far from a hardship posting, it was a city that was hard to leave, with many extending their stay years beyond the time envisaged in their original contracts.

This was a new perspective on Burma, but still, I couldn't imagine the country would be for me. Its ruling generals were notoriously paranoid and xenophobic, and all internal media was heavily censored. Burmese journalists who had overstepped the mark were among the more than two thousand political prisoners languishing in jail. Foreign journalists were banned from reporting, although occasionally they were invited as groups on organised trips during which they would be under the constant watch of government minders. I couldn't work freely in Burma, and however appealing our friends made it sound, I suppose I had discounted it as a place where I could ever live.

❧ ✿ ✿ ✿ ✿ ✿ ❧

A few years later and I was closer, living in neighbouring Thailand. Dan's job had taken us there, and we had a small child in tow. With this new proximity, I became intrigued about what lay across the border: Burma was just an hour's flight away, barely reported and apparently in deep slumber next to its booming neighbours. 'Nothing's ever going to happen there,' a veteran Bangkok-based journalist told me, fed up of waiting for the moment of change that had been periodically predicted since a failed 1988 uprising. I was keen to see for myself, and started to research a few feature stories that I might pursue if I travelled there undercover. One morning, in August 2007, I took my passport down to the Embassy of the Republic of the Union of Myanmar on a quiet Bangkok backstreet and applied for a visa, just to be prepared. I returned three days later and collected my passport with its blurry, purple-inked visa stamp. By luck, it was perfect journalistic timing: within weeks the Buddhist monks were on the march – the start of the Saffron Uprising. The embassy swiftly clamped down on visas. While frustrated foreign correspondents saw their applications flatly refused, I found myself on my way to Burma for the first time.

✿ ✿ ✿ ✿ ✿ ✿ ✿

My second arrival in Burma, like the first, was in circumstances I could not have anticipated. A few months after the uprising and its brutal dismissal, Burma returned to the international news headlines. In May 2008, Cyclone Nargis struck the Irrawaddy Delta, whose inhabitants were tragically unprepared to withstand a storm of such magnitude. The recovery operation was on a huge scale, and would continue for several years. Dan was offered a position running his organisation's relief and rehabilitation programme in the delta, to be based in Rangoon. It was an important opportunity for him, and I didn't take much persuading. Burma had an enigmatic attraction, and I was ready for something new.

In Burma I had a dual identity. Ostensibly, I was a typical 'trailing spouse', happy for the opportunity to spend time with my children in an exotic location. Our house was right next to the Australian diplomatic club, with a tennis court, gym and navy-tiled swimming pool. At the club's Sunday barbecues, the Burmese bar tender mixed rum sours for us to sip on the wooden verandah as our children played on the lawn. It was an idyllic life. But I also wanted to report, however challenging it would be. I thought of myself as a seasoned journalist, able to deliver from the toughest of environments. In the pursuit of news stories I had trekked across the baking scrubland of Southern Sudan, crossed the Hindu Kush on horseback and camped out in the Iraqi desert. The quiet backwater of Burma, I reasoned, should not pose too many problems.

I settled on my pseudonym, Phoebe Kennedy, a combination of the names of my niece and my grandmother. I found this degree of separation instantly liberating, Phoebe was to have all the adventures while the real me maintained her cover. I created numerous secret email accounts and identified the safest places from which to file my stories. Compared to other foreign reporters, who struggled to secure even short-term visas, I was in a wonderfully privileged situation in a notoriously inaccessible country.

But as well as privileged, I felt compromised. Simply not being able to tell people I was a journalist left me tongue-tied and frustrated. I had never had to hide my real identity or intentions before; in fact, being a journalist had generally been a positive, even in the most fragile situations. In Burma, I couldn't approach government officials, academics or business leaders; meetings with opposition activists carried risks on both sides. I was there under the aegis of my husband's aid organisation, and a false move on my part could have threatened its operations. As a foreigner, my conversations with locals could attract the scrutiny of Military Intelligence agents; if they were willing to chance that, my interviewees would have to trust me to change names and details that could identify them. On-the-record interviews were limited to diplomats or foreigners working for UN agencies. As a nervous, undercover journalist, I carried out some of the lamest *vox pop* interviews of my career on the streets of Rangoon – trying to fall into conversation with people in shops or on the streets in a quest for snippets that could liven up my articles.

During three years in Burma, I wrote for the *Independent*, for whom I had reported on the Saffron Uprising and whose foreign editors had a keen interest in Burma and Aung San Suu Kyi. Such was Suu Kyi's international celebrity, even if my stories weren't about her, she was invariably included as a point of reference. The accepted narrative of Burma was constructed through the prism of a struggle between the imprisoned Suu Kyi and the ruling generals, a simple story of good versus evil. Of course, it was more complicated than that, but many of the finer nuances were lost amidst a dearth of verifiable information. As the unwinding of Burma's long dictatorship began in March 2011, the boundaries within which the media had operated gradually started to be redrawn. For a long time, however, it was not clear where the new limits lay. 'We slowly started to push the door to see how far it would open,' Burmese journalist Zayar Hlaing told me. The reforms of the new government (led by general-turned-civilian president Thein Sein) were met with suspicion at first, especially by the international media. For a while, we foreign reporters clung mistrustfully to our pen names, until it became clear that new freedoms of expression were a genuine dividend of Burma's troubled political transition.

Frustratingly for me, these changes began to take root just as the time came for us to leave Burma. Packing up for departure, I had a nagging sense of business unfinished, of stories untold. Limited by the constraints of my clandestine professional life, I felt that the sum of my journalism had failed to articulate the richness of my experience in Burma – the fortitude, the kindness and the beauty. I could have done more. From this sense of incompleteness grew the kernel of this book, a snapshot of the lives of some of the people I had encountered during my stay. Some I knew very well, some I had met on just a few occasions. Many of the stories were recorded in my notebooks or are based on interviews stored as audio files on my computer. Some I had committed to memory. To me, all of my subjects, from Aung San Suu Kyi to the migrant worker Mu Mu, are remarkable characters. Together, I hope their stories provide an alternative perspective on Burma as it moves through these extraordinary times.

# 1
# The Storm

Zayar talked fast and sometimes I had trouble understanding him. We were sitting in the Parisien Café on the central Rangoon street where the soldiers had gunned down protesters a year before. Stalls selling betel leaves, cigarettes and steaming noodles elbowed for space next to hulking yellow and red generators that juddered into action each time the municipal power grid failed. I had just crossed the road using the concrete footbridge, home to a one-legged beggar with a cardboard sign and a six-year-old girl wearing a filthy nylon cardigan buttoned over her bare chest. She was sitting by an unfenced thirty-foot drop with a sticky-eyed baby on her lap, and signalled to me that they were both hungry by putting her hand to her mouth and then waving her open palm and shaking her head. I handed her some grubby *kyat* banknotes. Beneath the bridge, lines of ancient buses exhaled puffs of gritty fumes.

We were on the café's mezzanine floor where there was no one about. A little ball bounced along the words on a karaoke screen in the corner, and the loud Burmese pop music gave us cover to talk. This was the first time Zayar and I had met, having been put in touch by an American journalist in Bangkok, but we had already skirmished over who would buy the drinks. As a foreigner in Burma, I was cast in the permanent role of 'guest' and therefore could not pay for anything. But this was a fancy place, and the coffees cost about one dollar each. The bill of two dollars would probably exceed Zayar's daily income as a junior reporter. I insisted on paying, but I wasn't sure that buying myself out of the guilt was worth the pain it inflicted on him.

He piled sugar into his latte and stirred it intently. He just needed a few minutes to recover. Then he was off, jabbering away in his proficient but sometimes hard-to-understand English. Zayar Hlaing was a young journalist who had cut his teeth reporting on the devastation wrought by Cyclone Nargis. He explained how difficult it was to be a journalist in Burma: the low pay, the patchy Internet access, the unobtainable luxury of a mobile phone. He explained about the damned censor, how limiting and distorting it was, how hard it was to tell the truth. As well as writing for a weekly Burmese newspaper, Zayar also helped foreign reporters visiting Rangoon, coming up with story ideas, setting up interviews and interpreting. Now he was going to help me. I trusted him immediately. To my amateurish eye, he didn't have the look of a government agent; he was smooth-skinned with a goatee beard, a simple but stylish dresser in graphite-rimmed glasses, a well-cut T-shirt, dark denim jeans and velvet flip-flops. He wore a canvas satchel across his chest. But more telling than how he looked was Zayar's commitment to telling Burma's story, so ardent it could not be fake. Our meeting put him in greater danger than me, but he seemed excited to take me out to report, and was brimming with ideas like a tour guide eager to show off his city.

*~ ✿ ✿ ✿ ✿ ✿ ~*

Six months earlier, on Friday 2 May 2008, Zayar had sat quietly as usual in the morning editorial meeting, his spiral-bound notebook and pen in hand. He was *Modern Weekly*'s most recent recruit, and had only written half a dozen stories. The small TV in the corner of the office was tuned to CNN, and a satellite image showed an angry grey swirl spinning over the Bay of Bengal. Computer-generated graphics indicated that the cyclone was on course to hit Burma's Irrawaddy Delta, the mouth of the mighty river that springs in the Himalayan foothills. The journalists swivelled round to look at the screen. Since the previous year's crushed uprising, the country had barely warranted a mention on international news channels. Now, the presenter informed them, a big storm was brewing, and headed for Burma.

*Modern Weekly*'s editor turned back to his team and asked for a volunteer to go to the delta. No one responded. 'I really wanted to go,' Zayar told me later. 'But I was just a junior reporter.' The editor asked each journalist in turn, and each mumbled an excuse. The editor's eyes landed on Zayar. The assignment was his. The editor ushered him into his office and closed the door. He gave the novice reporter his mobile, the newspaper's only mobile phone, which at that time in Burma was worth $2,500, the most expensive item Zayar had ever handled. The editor clicked open the safe behind his desk and pulled out two lakh:

two small bricks of dirty 1,000 kyat notes, each bundle equivalent to around $200, about seven times Zayar's monthly salary. Zayar was to go home, pack a spare set of clothes, a torch, and tell his wife he would be gone for three or four days.

He arrived back at his ten-by-fifteen foot, one-room apartment near Rangoon's port just before lunchtime. His wife Aye Aye was at home with their baby daughter, sitting on their woven bamboo sleeping mat. The room was in a 1920s tenement block built by the Scottish-run Burmah Oil Company for its labourers. In the corner there was a single water tap and a gas ring run off a cylinder that served as a kitchen. Zayar's books and newspapers were stacked up against the wall, and next to them a small area had been set aside for their modest collection of baby paraphernalia, a pile of pink and white clothes, special soft towels and tenderly folded blankets with appliquéd teddy bear faces. Just a week after the birth, Aye Aye had gone back to work at the accounts department of the Myanmar Port Authority, taking her daughter with her in a Moses basket. But today the baby was feverish, and Aye Aye had decided to stay at home. Zayar stuffed a few things into a small rucksack, wrapping the money, phone and his camera inside his clothes. Repeating his editor's words, he told his wife he would be away for three or four days. 'I told her I was going to the delta. I told her not to worry,' Zayar said. 'She didn't say anything.'

✿ ✿ ✿ ✿ ✿ ✿

Excited to be on his first proper assignment, Zayar boarded a bus to the city of Pathein. The single-lane highway connecting Rangoon with Burma's fourth city skirts the top of the Irrawaddy Delta. As the bus juddered over patches of hand-broken stones awaiting their tarmac coating, the passengers looked from the windows with increasing alarm at palm trees bent almost double by the strengthening wind. The frowning driver, a cigarette lodged in the corner of his mouth, gripped the wheel as southerly gusts buffeted the left side of his bus. As it grew dark a tree branch crashed on to the windscreen, its limbed silhouette clinging on for a second, and flung away. The passengers gasped, then quietened, staring ahead, some gripping the headrests in front of them, others thumbing strings of smooth, jade beads.

It was late evening by the time Zayar arrived. His head down, clutching his rucksack to his chest, he battled his way through torrents of rain and winds that nearly lifted him off his feet. He banged on the door of a guesthouse close to the bus terminal. The power had cut out. The wind rattled the thin glass in the windows as Zayar sat alone in the candlelit dining room and ate a plate of cold chicken curry and rice. He went to his room and lay on the narrow hard bed, listening to the angry noises: a howl through the slatted glass of his window, a distant, ominous rumbling, a bang and a crash from outside. The square, concrete building trembled in its shallow foundations. Zayar slept fitfully for a few hours, waking with the light. He sat up, fully clothed, grabbed his bag and went out to the street.

In the calm after the storm, unrested residents emerged from their houses to survey the damage. Motorbikes had been tossed on their sides and up the street, trees sixty or seventy years old had been toppled, along with telegraph poles and road signs. Corrugated tin sheeting had been ripped from roofs; the storm had sheared tarpaulin awnings. There were days of clearing up ahead, but lying just north of the cyclone's direct path Pathein had survived without major damage. The bustling city would soon be up and running again, minus its shady green foliage. Zayar made his way to the police station. He wanted to know the extent of the damage deeper into the delta, closer to the ocean. Phone and power lines were down, but there had been some radio traffic. The police had a report from Hainggyi Island, at Burma's south-western-most tip. It had been badly hit, the police officer said, dozens, maybe hundreds of people killed. That was where Zayar would head for next.

He wandered down to the banks of the Pathein River, one of the distributaries of the Irrawaddy that glides through paddy fields and mangrove swamps to the Bay of Bengal. The riverbank was already crowded with people, worried about relatives downstream, trying to hire boats. The boatmen, inspecting the damage to their battered vessels, refused all offers, even an inflated bid from Zayar, who had the newspaper's cash in his rucksack. An ocean liner was grounded on the far side; the water was littered with the flotsam of the storm. Zayar waited on the muddy bank, sprinting off with the pack at each false rumour that a boat would sail. He offered around cigarettes and chatted, memorising what people were telling him. In the fraught atmosphere, he didn't want to risk taking notes. There was no phone signal. His expensive mobile was useless. At mid-morning, around five dozen soldiers – sleeves rolled up, khaki trousers tucked into black leather boots – came trotting along the brow of the bank. Their commander, picking his way through the debris-strewn mud with the aid of a stick, brought up the rear, barking orders. The soldiers clambered down the sticky slope to the jetties to talk to the boatmen. Each bare-chested, *longyi*-clad sailor shook his head and pointed further up the bank. There was shouting, a huddle, the commander came down to seal the deal. 'It only took them a few minutes,' Zayar said. 'The soldiers commandeered a boat. They didn't pay.' Hainggyi Island was home to a naval base, and the troops had orders to inspect the damage. Despite what was already emerging as a major disaster, there was no other relief effort taking shape on the riverbank from this, the delta's second major port. Survivors of the storm would be left to fend for themselves.

It looked like a two-hundred-foot barge, used usually to transport rice, would be the only vessel sailing that day, and the anxious crowd clamoured to get on board. Zayar elbowed his way forward, leapt from the jetty, had a quick word in the ear of the ship's captain (dropping a few names from the Port Authority) and secured his spot on deck, squatting down, hugging his rucksack. Others clambered from the listing wooden pier, frantic, heaving with them jerry cans of water and sacks of rice. They kept on coming until the tense, sweating captain yelled at them to stop, and the rifle-bearing soldiers manhandled them back on to the jetty. There were shouts and recriminations from the bank as the young deck hands untethered the ropes. At 1 p.m., the ship drifted from its moorings under a porcelain blue sky, the water calm, the air fresh and still.

❧ ✿✿✿✿✿ ☙

They arrived at midnight. There was silence on the deck, silence on shore. From the helm the captain switched on a powerful searchlight and directed it towards the land. Everyone on deck stared outwards. Dead quiet. Then a woman stepped into the beam, elderly, scrawny, bare-shouldered, a sarong knotted at her chest. She stared into the light, at the ship she couldn't see. 'Our island looks like a graveyard!' she cried. The light was cut. In darkness, no one dared leave the ship. For another five hours, the passengers crouched on deck, in intermittent slumber.

Then the blackness turned to faint violet as the sun began to rise from the ocean behind, gradually bathing the destruction in front of them in a golden glow. Felled trees, shattered timber-framed houses, the angular outlines of dislocated objects were smothered in a coating of brownish-black mud. Two broken, wooden fishing boats were perched on high ground at the back of what would have been the beach. The woman had gone; there was not a single sign of life.

Cyclone Nargis was a Category Four tropical storm that raged in from the Bay of Bengal and hit the south-western tip of the Irrawaddy Delta on the evening of 2 May. Its ferocious winds roared through rural villages, flattening the delta's bamboo and thatch structures built on stilts above the networks of silty brown waterways. The power of the cyclone drove walls of seawater up the tidal rivers that drain the Irrawaddy into the Indian Ocean. Thousands of people were swept away in the surge water, their infants snatched from their grasp. Along the coast, the only people who survived were those who were able to cling to trees or pieces of floating debris, sometimes for ten hours or more. When the waters receded, they found their clothes had been ripped from their bodies; some had burn-like injuries from the force of the rain, cuts and broken bones. As stunned survivors staggered around like drunkards, looking for scraps of clothes to cover themselves, bodies slipped from trees and thudded to the ground. It was weeks before the number of dead was calculated.

On the shore of Hainggyi Island, the jetties had been smashed and swept out to sea. The ship hands threw wooden gangplanks on to the sludge to help the passengers disembark – soldiers first, with bags of rice to be delivered to what remained of the naval camp. With six bottles of water in his rucksack, Zayar clambered after them, removing his flip-flops and rolling up his jeans. The group gazed around at a disorienting landscape where everything was in the wrong place. Coconut trees were uprooted; big tamarind trees, their trunks the width of four people, had been snapped like matchsticks. Upturned fishing boats had been tossed into the island's interior, one thrown on top of one of the few standing buildings – a wood and brick Buddhist monastery. The tangled roots of mangroves sat on the surface like nests of snakes, as if eased up by a giant pitchfork. The air heated quickly with the sun, and a sweet, putrid smell seethed from the mud-covered ground. Rice fields were flooded with reddish-brown water, receding in the heat to reveal the twisted limbs of bodies dumped by the storm surge. All the island's woven rattan houses had been obliterated. Survivors were few. Having received warnings about the magnitude of the storm by shortwave radio, naval camp personnel had managed to retreat to a school – a concrete building and the sturdiest on the island. The school lost its roof but mostly survived the battering, sheltering the naval unit, some special branch officers and their families, and a few dozen other fortunate islanders.

The lieutenant colonel was a very fat man and, as Zayar recalled, very relaxed after the ordeal of the previous night. Even in the wake of a disaster, Zayar knew he had to abide by the rules, and he had come to ask the most senior officer on the island for permission to report. He was conjuring up strategies to counter the blanket 'no' he was expecting. The lieutenant colonel, in a dark green uniform, a leather belt buckled high around his tummy, was sitting on a folding chair at one end of a trestle table in what had now become Hainggyi Island's makeshift command centre. His radio was on the table in front of him, alongside parcels of the mild stimulant betel nut, wrapped in its green leaves. The betel juices had stained black outlines on the soldier's teeth, and he intermittently leaned to the side to spit blood-red juices on to the floor. He laughed when Zayar made his request, and told him there was nothing to see. 'But there is only one boat, and it doesn't leave till evening,' Zayar said, evenly. 'Maybe I can spend my time looking around, to see what has happened, to see if any help is possible.' The commander leaned back in his chair and sneered. He clicked his fingers and summoned a special branch officer whose motorbike had miraculously survived the storm. 'He will take you,' he told Zayar.

Zayar spent seven hours on the ghostly island, picking through debris and mud; the motorbike was of little use. Stunned survivors, half-naked, begged him for water. Wells and fresh water ponds had been inundated with salt water, and everyone was suffering a terrible thirst. Survivors drank coconut milk to stay alive, eating coconut flesh and grains of wet rice retrieved from the receding surge water. There were countless tales of families decimated, just one or two survivors left. The storm waters had carried most of the bodies out into the now calm, lapping Indian Ocean. The heat grew intense. As Zayar clambered over the debris, a nail pierced his rubber sandal, cutting the sole of his foot.

The scene Zayar witnessed on Hainggyi Island was being played out in hundreds of villages across the Irrawaddy Delta. This was a disaster of epic proportions: tens of thousands had died, and hundreds of thousands of people were in need of urgent assistance. Children, dumbstruck by fear and trauma, wandered alone. Young women cowered in the undergrowth among dead bodies, calling out for scraps of clothes to be passed to them so they could stagger out. The injured and elderly cried out for water. But Burma's military government, already infamous for its heartless treatment of its citizens, responded to the disaster with callousness of a new magnitude. Or, more accurately, did not respond. There was no coordinated relief operation in the delta. The generals turned down offers of assistance from foreign governments, denied clearance to aid flights, and even turned back the planes packed with relief materials and aid workers that did manage to land at Rangoon airport. Astoundingly, a referendum to vote on the junta's newly drawn-up constitution went ahead as scheduled on 10 May, eight days after the cyclone, in all but the worst-affected areas. It took Senior General Than Shwe a further week to emerge from the country's brand new, unscathed capital Naypyidaw to visit the disaster zone, and then only to inspect nervous 'survivors' at a pristine Potemkin refugee camp which had been hastily constructed for his benefit.

With little or no help from Burma's government (or its half-million-strong standing army, the Tatmadaw), the first tasks of survival were organised by the survivors themselves. Communities – what remained of them – spontaneously formed action groups, led by monks or teachers, to bury bodies, clear debris, care for children and share out what few resources they could scavenge. In Rangoon and Pathein, residents started to organise their own aid convoys, loading water, food, medicines and tarpaulins into cars and trucks and driving down to the delta. To the Burmese people, this self-sufficiency was nothing new – it was how they had operated for half a century. During years of corrupt and inept military governance, the people of Burma had devised their own coping mechanisms. 'I've come to the conclusion that when something bad is happening to a society, it binds the people together,' the head of a Burmese community organisation told me. 'They want to help each other. People can't rely on the government, so we have to make our own safety net.' And so it was. After Burma's biggest catastrophe in more than a century, the humanitarian workers were the survivors themselves.

After some weeks, however, there was progress. In an agreement brokered by UN Secretary General Ban Ki-moon, Than Shwe agreed to allow aid agencies into the delta. The Senior General was under diplomatic pressure from Burma's South-east Asian neighbours, and seemed to have been shocked into action by the Chinese government's swift response to the massive Sichuan earthquake that struck central China ten days after Nargis. In contrast to Than Shwe and his leisurely approach, Chinese Premier Wen Jiabao was on a plane to the earthquake zone ninety minutes after it had struck. China dispatched emergency medical teams, mobilised tens of thousands of troops to assist in the recovery operation, and soon declared three days of mourning. On 20 May, eighteen days after the cataclysmic storm, Burma declared its own mourning period of three days – for the dead whose numbers would eventually be estimated at 138,000. But the regime's efforts were little, and late. Its dereliction of duty would not be forgotten, and many Burma watchers believed that the leadership's signal failure to deal with the disaster helped to contribute to the demise of military rule – at least in this, its most autocratic, merciless incarnation.

❧ ✿ ✿ ✿ ✿ ✿ ❦

The long, low moo of the ship's horn sounded across the island just before 2 p.m. Zayar, on the back of the special branch officer's motorbike, bumped around obstacles back to the beach. He was in pain from the cut in his foot, and had started to run a fever. He had given away all his water and dried food and grabbed a coconut as sustenance for the journey home. The barge cast off for the slow voyage back upstream to Pathein. There was silence on board, as the bloated carcasses of humans, pigs and dogs drifted by in the murky water. When darkness fell it was a dense, starless night, and Zayar could see no more of the deathly landscape. He sat motionless on the deck, listening for the faint tinkling of bells as other ships signalled their approach. In his head he concocted his article, his first, terrible scoop.

Forty-eight hours later, his bus had reached Hlaing Thar Yar terminal on the western edge of Rangoon. The city was in total darkness. Tree trunks and lampposts lay across the streets. When Zayar managed to flag down a taxi, the driver charged him triple the usual fare to his home. 'It was only then that I realised the cyclone had hit Rangoon,' Zayar said.

'In all that time I didn't even consider it.' The driver dropped him near the port. 'This was the place I had lived all my life, but I didn't recognise anything. The trees were gone. There was no electricity at all.'

Eventually, he found the small lane that led to his quarters. He stumbled through the mud and debris, feeling his way with his hands along the brick wall. The cut in his foot stung. He found his room – a tree had crashed into its tiled roof. He was standing in ankle-deep water. He tried to open the door; it was jammed. 'I shouted in the dark: "Where is my family?" Suddenly I was scared.' He heard a soft cry from his neighbour's house. His wife. 'I found her with the neighbour, sitting on the bed with our baby. "Where have you been?" she whispered.' Zayar sat with her for a while, holding her hand, but his mind was elsewhere. He asked his neighbour for three candles and some paper. He cleared a space on the floor and sat down, cross-legged, to write his story. He wrote and wrote and fell asleep without finishing. In the morning, he picked up his papers and took them to the office and typed up his story. His editor read over his shoulder, making a few suggestions. The other journalists were working on their reports of the situation in Rangoon, but it was clear that it would be Zayar's story on the front page. *Modern Weekly*'s deadline was at noon, to give time for the articles to be read by the censor. Miraculously, Zayar's was passed, with just a few deletions, and was published the next day. His home was flooded, his belongings destroyed, and his wife Aye Aye was in silent trauma. But Zayar, the junior reporter, had produced one of the first reports of the disaster in the delta.

# 2
# Border Crossings

We were packing, and down to those drawers that are always left till last: the ones containing old mobile phone chargers, unidentified keys, business cards, paper clips and bits of Blu-Tack. We had been in this Bangkok house for less than three years, but still the stuff had built up. There were boxes for things we were taking, boxes for things we were giving away, and the black bin bags were supposed to be for things we were throwing out. Not much was making it to the throw-out pile. Every time I tried to put something in a bin bag, Mu Mu would grab it from me. 'No, I can use it!' she said of a nearly finished bottle of shampoo or a child's T-shirt stained beyond hope. The kitchen table was piling up with rejected belongings – a broken hairdryer, a carved wooden candle holder and half a bag of self-raising flour – that the husband of Mu Mu's friend Mie was going to pick up later in a rented tuk-tuk.

It was an odd situation. Mu Mu, our Burmese nanny who had worked for us since we arrived in Thailand, was helping us pack and leave, and we were dreading saying goodbye to her. As much as we wanted to take her with us, she had told us she couldn't come. The trouble was, this new country we were moving to was Mu Mu's home. And she didn't want to go back. It was June 2008, a few weeks after the cyclone. Aid agencies were now thinking about the long-term rehabilitation of the devastated Irrawaddy Delta, and my husband had been offered the opportunity to move to Rangoon to help run his aid organisation's recovery programme. I had only caught a brief glimpse of Burma on my reporting trip a year before. It still felt exotic, remote and untouchable. Now I had the chance to live there.

We liked to think of Mu Mu as one of the family, but this move highlighted the gaping differences between us. We had choices, she didn't. For us it was an adventure, a few years in a tropical backwater, in a city we already knew was quieter and more pleasant than Bangkok. We knew expats who lived on the lake in Rangoon and would sit out on their terraces with evening drinks to watch orange and purple streaks of sunset reflected in the water. For holidays, we could enjoy the temples at Pagan, the beaches at Ngapali, the floating markets of Inle Lake. And when we felt like it, we could go home. For Mu Mu it wasn't so simple. I already knew her story, with its hardship and heartbreak, and I could understand why a posting in Rangoon might not hold quite the same appeal for her.

❧ ✿ ✿ ✿ ✿ ✿ ❧

When I first met Mu Mu she was nineteen, but she told me she was twenty-three. I'm fairly sure that was the only untruth she told me when I interviewed her for a job as a nanny for our daughter. It was January 2006 and we were sitting in an air-conditioned, serviced apartment on the twenty-second floor of a block in the middle of Bangkok's shopping district. I was a new mother of a six-month-old baby girl, and our small family had just arrived from London for my husband to take up a new job with an international aid agency. There was no way I could have afforded childcare in London, but in Bangkok, as I had discovered from my brief experience of the city's expatriate mother–toddler groups, everyone had 'help'. The nannies – usually unglamorous girls from rural Thailand or across the border in Burma – wore fake Hello Kitty T-shirts, stonewashed jeans and flip-flops, or their employers' cast-offs. They would accompany the family on shopping expeditions or to playgroups, and made an art of knowing when their 'madam' required them to entertain the children or melt into the background. They would push trolleys around supermarkets as their employers chucked in the groceries and would sit at restaurant tables spooning food into children's mouths while the mothers gossiped or whined about their domestic staff right there in front of them. They knew their employers liked them to be as invisible as possible, which was confirmed to me at a pay-at-the-door children's swimming party at Bangkok's British Club. At the entrance two expat women sat behind a table selling tickets. 'Do we pay for our maids?' asked one mother, as her nanny, beads of sweat springing on her forehead, dragged a child's buggy up the steps. 'No need, we don't count them as actual people,' smirked the organising lady. So often, the girls who cleaned our apartments and loved our children were treated with suspicion and contempt, a response perhaps to the devotion our children felt for their gentle carers. Mothers felt threatened. One expatriate housewife boasted to me about how she had torn up her Burmese nanny's work permit – the only identity and security she would have had – because she suspected the girl of stealing money. Another had installed a secret camera and found her maid 'lying on my bed, reading my magazines!' when she ought to have been mopping the floor.

Mu Mu may have lied about her age (she told me months later that she didn't think I would have employed her had I known how young she was, and she was probably right), but she was truthful about already having been a domestic worker in the Thai capital for nearly five years. She was barely fifteen when she walked out of Burma and across jungled mountains to elude Thai border guards. A broker bundled her into a pickup truck, where she had to lie on her side, packed in with around thirty others, two layers of tarpaulin thrown over them, for the suffocating journey to Bangkok. Her first job, with a middle-class Thai family in the Bangkok suburbs, came with a salary of twenty-five dollars a month. She spent her days sweeping floors, cleaning toilets, scrubbing and wringing out piles of laundry by hand. She massaged the feet of her mistresses, ironed 'sir's' underpants and groomed the dogs. By the time she came to work for us, she had already looked after nine children, often sleeping at night in their bedrooms so their parents wouldn't be disturbed if the infants woke. When not needed in the children's room she had slept in the servants' quarters – a windowless, airless cupboard which was a standard feature of every middle-class Bangkok apartment.

A position as an undocumented domestic worker in Thailand is no dream job, yet every year thousands of Burmese girls made exactly the same trip across the border as Mu Mu. Some found themselves in much worse situations. Tricked by brokers to expect work as waitresses or nannies, they would end up in the brothels of Bangkok and Pattaya, trapped in bonded labour, often for years, until they had paid back 'debts' to agents. Without passports or visas, they were illegal migrants and at the mercy of Thai police. If caught, they would have to pay bribes, endure verbal abuse and even sexual attacks. Yet every month, it seemed, another of Mu Mu's friends arrived, then two cousins, then her younger sister. It never really made sense to me. What on earth could life be like in Burma to make the prospects in Bangkok – domestic servitude at best, sexual slavery at worst – enticing? It was something I asked Mu Mu many times. From her story, and those of others I would meet, I learned far more about life in Burma than I did covering the big news events that made headlines at home.

*~ ✿ ✿ ✿ ✿ ✿ ~*

Mu Mu was born in 1986 and grew up in Hpa'an, a vibrant market town in eastern Burma set amidst the limestone escarpments and emerald paddy fields of Karen state. The Karen, a hill tribe that traces its origins to Mongolia, is one of Burma's largest ethnic groups, with its own language, calendar and traditional dress – brightly coloured embroidered tunics and matching scarves tied at the side of the head. The Karen consider themselves different, separate from the majority Burmans, and took up arms practically from the moment Burma won independence from Britain in 1948. The Karen National Union (KNU) rebel group took control of much of the eastern part of Karen state, along the border with Thailand. When she was growing up, Mu Mu's family suffered harassment from soldiers on both sides. As a small girl she would hide behind her mother's legs when rebel fighters turned up at the family's smallholding on Hpa'an's rural fringe, demanding rice, whisky and a place to sleep. Her mother would lay down extra bamboo sleeping mats for them. After dinner, the yellow flame of the oil lamp would be doused, and the soldiers would lie down to sleep with the family in their single-roomed shack. Mu Mu woke at sunrise and watched the men snoring, open-mouthed, glistening with boozy sweat, their guns at their sides. 'There were always problems. The next day the government soldiers would come and say, "Why are you keeping Karen soldiers here?" Both sides were trouble for us.' By the time she had started school, Mu Mu's family had moved to a wooden house on a main street in town, where government troops were firmly in charge.

Mu Mu, a pretty, playful child, was the second of four daughters. Her father worked for the state-owned firm that controlled all sales of liquor in the town. Although his salary was low, less than thirty dollars per month, the position gave him the opportunity to supplement his income with 'tea money' – backhanders from alcohol producers and shopkeepers who needed to keep the middleman on side. Her mother had a small shop in the front room of their house, selling eggs, little snacks and packets of instant noodles. They were poor, but Mu Mu didn't feel it. 'My friends were the same like us. No TV, no nothing.

But my grandfather still had a farm, so we didn't need to buy rice or vegetables. We always had enough to eat.' Dressed in a white shirt and green sarong-style skirt, she went to the local government school. She wasn't a particularly talented student, unlike her studious elder sister, but her academic achievements were thwarted by external forces. Mu Mu thinks she may be ill-starred; she has certainly had her share of bad luck.

❧ ✿ ✿ ✿ ✿ ✿ ❦

On a cool, clear February morning, just weeks after the turn of the millennium, Mu Mu was cycling her big-wheeled, one-gear bike, on her way to sit her first high school matriculation examination. Her uniform was washed and pressed, her shiny black hair was neatly tied back in a ponytail. On each of her cheeks was a finger sweep of *thanaka*, the yellowish tree bark paste that serves as both make-up and sunscreen. Her steel tiffin tin containing a simple lunch of rice, fish paste and fried greens hung from the handlebar. The road ran quietly through neatly tended rice fields, a ridge of steep chalk hills studded with golden stupas rising up to the right. Mu Mu was contemplating the history exam that awaited her when a buffalo reared up out of the paddy and into the road. She swerved, lost balance and ended up in a ditch with a broken arm. She missed the examinations and was not permitted to re-sit.

In Burma, the matriculation or 'Tenth Standard' exams determine a student's future at the age of just fifteen or sixteen. The Burmese education system has little interest in a student's vocation or passion; it is all about grades. Those with the highest marks are expected to go on to study medicine at university, regardless of their desire to care for the sick. Slightly lower grades will steer the student towards the engineering or law faculties, after that come languages and computer science. Zoology and history departments are traditionally populated by students who have not excelled in their high school exams. Passing 'Tenth Standard' is regarded as a minimum educational requirement in Burmese society; without it, it is difficult to secure any employment beyond menial work. More than a decade on, Mu Mu still felt the sting of failure. 'I am ashamed that I didn't pass Tenth Standard,' she said. 'Even now, I don't like to talk about it. I feel that I am not educated, I am not clever.'

The accident couldn't have been more badly timed. The atmosphere at home was becoming more and more fraught. A year earlier, Mu Mu's father had lost his government job. The family had tried to survive by renting out their prized asset, their telephone line, which allowed locals to call their relatives who had left for Thailand, Malaysia and Singapore in search of work. It kept their head above water for a few months, until the State Peace and Development Council changed the rules. In those days before the Internet, when mobile phones were restricted to a small elite, the junta still had control of its citizens' ability to communicate with the wider world. They wanted to keep it that way. New regulations were abruptly introduced so international calls could only be made on sanctioned phones and the family's fledgling business died. 'At home everything was bad. My father and mother were fighting the whole time, and he was always saying bad things to me. "What can you do now you have failed Tenth Standard?" I felt like I was a problem.' Mu Mu could only think of one solution. Her cousin had recently come back from Bangkok for a visit, and was about to return to Thailand. Mu Mu begged to go with her.

Mu Mu had only made one trip out of Hpa'an before, a one-day school visit to Rangoon. She packed her few belongings in a small rucksack, her clothes, some soap and a toothbrush. There were no photographs at home she could take, no mementos or books. She had no passport and no money – the trip would cost 8,000 Thai baht, about $250, to be funded by a broker who smuggled migrants across the Thai border and on to Bangkok. This would be paid back through her wages as a domestic worker, 'a maid', as her cousin called it. Mu Mu couldn't imagine her future life, she had no idea what to expect. She couldn't envisage the Bangkok apartments that her cousin had described, ten, fifteen, even twenty floors up. She had never lived anywhere with running water or an inside toilet, she had never seen a skyscraper, she had never been in a lift.

There were no special goodbyes. Her parents were fractious, preoccupied. Her sisters had their own concerns. 'I left the house as if I was going to the market.' With her cousin, Mu Mu caught a bus to the border town of Myawaddy, where they met their broker, a skinny woman with gold jewellery and heavy make-up. Getting across the border to the Thai town of Mae Sot was easy: the guards had been paid off. But after that it would become tricky. Thai police were on patrol to stem the flow of illegal migrants heading for the lights of Bangkok. 'We set off at night through the mountains. We had to go by foot for a long way so that we would join the road again further down, past all the gates, the checkpoints.' For five nights they were on the move, a column of around forty or fifty people, like an army brigade. They hid by day and trekked in darkness, herded by a group of armed men. Mu Mu doesn't know who they were. 'The people who took us were very strict, very rough. If they say you move, you move.' They were still in Karen territory, now on the Thai side of the border. In daylight they hid in farmers' cattle sheds, each day receiving a polythene bag of cooked rice, dripping with condensation. At night they were on the move, plagued by mosquitoes and leeches, drinking water from streams. On the fifth night the group came to a deserted house. It was boarded up and looked empty. They were ushered inside. In the gloom they could make out the shapes of dozens more people, squatting on the floor in silence, waiting. There Mu Mu put on the jeans her cousin had brought for her, the first pair she had ever worn. It was time for the human cargo to be packed into pickups, for the drive to the city.

☙ ✿ ✿ ✿ ✿ ✿ ❧

Mu Mu was beautiful. She looked like a Sioux princess. She had a strong mouth and perfect, straight, white teeth, the product of cheap Darlie toothpaste rather than fancy orthodontic treatment. She had a regal, straight nose and cheekbones so high they were all you could see from most angles of her profile. Her cat's eyes slanted upwards to her temples, and on special occasions she would accentuate their startling shape with a modest stroke of black eyeliner. She was slender, with the sort of waist you could reach around with two hands. But she was oddly proportioned, her legs much too short for her torso. This, I discovered (not from her), was a sign of stunting. Although she was rarely hungry, Mu Mu grew up in deep poverty. Her staple meals of rice and vegetables from her grandfather's plot were often devoid of protein. She just didn't get the nutrition she needed to reach the full height that nature had intended for her.

Mu Mu had a boyfriend called Saw Myo, something she proudly told me at our first meeting. Saw Myo was a Karen boy from her hometown who had also come to Thailand in search of a brighter future. Their families knew each other a little, but she had only really got to know him in Bangkok. Living away from home had allowed young Burmese to circumvent the cultural norms of their society, in which a public courtship must culminate quickly in marriage to safeguard the reputation of the girl and her family. Mu Mu met Saw Myo when she was seventeen, through mutual friends on Sunday, her 'off', when the Hpa'an community would gather at the Karen Baptist church in Bangkok, the social highlight of the week. Nineteenth-century missionaries had scored some of their greatest successes among the Karen people of Burma's eastern hills; the provision of education and healthcare had been rewarded with high rates of conversion. Consequently, Karen state has a much higher concentration of Christians than much of mainly Buddhist, lowland Burma. When Mu Mu took a job which did not require her to 'live in', she and Saw Myo moved in together in a hot, airless Bangkok bedsit, something her parents back in Hpa'an fiercely disapproved of, but given Mu Mu's status as the family breadwinner they could do nothing about. 'They could say a lot of words, but they had no power,' Mu Mu said.

I never met him, but Mu Mu showed me pictures of Saw Myo on her phone. He was not what I expected, he wore thick spectacles, his cap of black hair was neatly parted. He looked a bit geeky. She told me he was thirteen years older than her and he loved books and computers. She clearly felt awed and outclassed by his supposed intellect. I asked her if she would like to get married to him. 'Now we are working to stay alive,' she said. 'We can't think about that right now.' But deep down Mu Mu must have believed that she would marry him one day. By the time she came to work for us, Saw Myo had left Bangkok. Mu Mu was cagey about it at first, but as her trust in me grew, she told me he was at the refugee camp on Thailand's border with Burma. Most of the Burmese domestic workers had friends and relatives in the camps, sprawling bamboo shanties dotted along the hillsides of Thailand's western border. Thai authorities banned the building of any permanent structures in the camps, so everything was constructed from wood, bamboo and tarpaulin. They were cities in themselves; helped by generous aid funding they had their own schools, clinics, shops and orphanages. Most of the refugees were from Burma's hill tribes – Karen, Mon and Shan. Many inhabitants had lived in the camps since 1984, when government forces launched a full-scale offensive against ethnic Karen insurgents, pushing ten thousand Karen refugees across the border. Some were dissidents from Rangoon and Mandalay who had escaped to Thailand following the failed uprisings of 1988, 1996 and 2007.

As the camps swelled, the United Nations established major resettlement programmes for the refugees, sending thousands each year to new homes in the United States, Canada, Norway and Australia. The lure of a new life in the West had attracted a new breed to the camp, migrants like Saw Myo, who had not fled directly from the barrel of a gun but instead from the poverty of opportunity that life in Burma offered its young people.

While not undeserving, Saw Myo and those like him did not meet the criteria set by the UN's refugee agency, the UNHCR, to join its resettlement programme. So in the interviews with UN officials they would lie. They knew they had to prove they had fled persecution, and although in some way each of them had, they knew they had to package their stories to tick the UN boxes. So they would each have their own tale of their village razed, of being chased through the jungle by Burmese soldiers, and swimming across the Moei River to safety in Thailand. (Most of them had used this route, but like Mu Mu, in a more calculated way, using brokers to bribe officials on both sides to smooth the way.) They memorised dates, times and detail so as not to be caught out during several rounds of screening. As a mostly Christian group, with an easily digestible story of oppression by an evil regime, the Karen were Washington's refugees of choice in the mid-2000s. Tens of thousands were extracted from the camps to start new lives in states such as Indiana, California and Texas.

After four years of poorly paid work in Bangkok, Saw Myo decided to head for Mae Ra Moe camp in the hills of northwest Thailand. He hoped to join the UN waiting list and follow his old schoolfriend who had just completed a week's training in 'Western ways' (how to use an upright, flushing toilet, eat with a knife and fork, apply for a driving licence and behave on a plane) before flying out to Vancouver. But Saw Myo found himself at the bottom of the list with a three-year wait ahead of him. By then, there would be no guarantee that the United States or Canada would still be as favourably disposed to the Karen refugees and willing to take them in such great numbers. In the rainy season the camp turned to mud. Living conditions were harsh, mosquitoes were a menace, there was no electricity and food was scarce. Saw Myo survived on UN rations of vegetables, beans, oil, salt and rice. There was no reliable mobile phone signal up in the hills and communication with Mu Mu became sporadic.

❧ ✿ ✿ ✿ ✿ ✿ ❧

I answered my phone in the baking sun of the car park of Villa supermarket on Thong Lor in Bangkok and tried to take in what he was telling me. 'Hello, ma'am, this is Saw Myo, I am the friend of Mu Mu.' His English was perfect, his tone courteous. I thought he was going to ask me a favour – for some money, a letter of reference. But no. 'Ma'am I need you to tell Mu Mu that I'm going to get married'

'What?' I didn't understand. Who to? 'But weren't you planning to marry *her*?'

'Marry Mu Mu? No, no, no,' he laughed as if to say marriage to a poor, uneducated, albeit beautiful, housemaid was never a possibility.

Saw Myo was going to marry a girl at the top of the waiting list. She would be his ticket to the West. I felt panicked, trying to take in what it all meant. Mu Mu would be devastated. I didn't want to be the one to tell her, and anyway, given I was her employer and Saw Myo and I had never met, it was an odd request. 'You have to tell her yourself,' I said.

It was a weekend, Mu Mu was in her shared, one–roomed apartment on the banks of a smelly *klong*, one of Bangkok's water arteries. When I got home my phone rang again. It was Mu Mu. Saw Myo had called her already.

'He will marry?' The last syllable was a squeak as she started to sob. 'I thought he would marry me!'

She came to our house. For once, the total suppression of her own needs and feelings, a manner she had perfected during years of domestic service, was cast aside. Normally when she spoke to me she would be obsessively tidying, bouncing the baby on her knee, or vigorously polishing a tap. Despite my repeatedly imploring her to eat with us at the table, she would always take her lunch to the back door, where she would sit cross-legged on the floor to eat. Now she was wailing, unguarded, ripping tissues from the box and flinging them used to the floor. She went over it and over it. She fell asleep that night on our sofa, heartbroken and exhausted.

By the next morning Mu Mu had a plan. She asked for time off and an advance on her salary. She was going to the camp to find him. 'My head was full of blood. I had to understand it. If I couldn't make sense of it, I felt that I couldn't stay in this world,' Mu Mu told me, years later. She now faced another dangerous journey across a country where she was an illegal immigrant. She hitched a lift to the border in a minibus with other Burmese workers, hiding on the floor as they passed through scrappy Thai market towns. It was a long, hot, bumpy ride, but Mu Mu felt no discomfort. 'At that time I didn't care if I lived or died.' She was deposited in the town of Mae Sot and made the last part of the journey on the back of a motorbike, up the winding road that led through the forested hills to Mae Ra Moe. Blinking the grit from her eyes, she saw the fence that ran round the camp, a bamboo and thatch city cut out of the hillside. It was late afternoon, ribbons of grey smoke from hundreds of charcoal braziers rose into the pale blue sky. Her head down, she followed her elongated shadow into the camp. Her sandals kicked up dust from the dirt path. She walked past the rows of wood and bamboo houses looking for faces she recognised. Shyly, she started to ask people for Saw Myo. In a camp of more than fifteen thousand refugees, Mu Mu was met with countless blank faces until, finally, someone told her where she might find him.

Saw Myo was sitting cross-legged inside the hut, chatting with a group of men. Mu Mu blocked the light in the doorway, and he looked up, through his thick glasses. Backlit, he could only make out her profile at first; he wasn't sure it was her. He stood up and came towards her. 'He was very angry,' Mu Mu said. 'He said, "What are you doing here?"' Mu Mu instantly dissolved into tears. 'I loved him because I was young. I only had him,' she told me. Saw Myo was obliged to explain to Mu Mu why he had ended their relationship. After the initial shock, he grew kinder. 'He said he had loved me, but our lives were going in different directions. He said we couldn't be together.' Later that evening, Mu Mu met Saw Myo's new fiancée, who had no knowledge of his past relationship. The girls sat and spoke quietly together. They had both known hardship and they recognised it in each other. It seemed a bond of solidarity grew. The next day, the girl called off the marriage, saying she needed time to think. Mu Mu spent three weeks in the camp, sleeping in the bamboo hut of her rival. It was December, freezing at night so high up in the hills. Mu Mu had never experienced a cold like it. Her body and mind were numb.

~ ✿✿✿✿✿ ~

Mu Mu came back to Bangkok and back to work. It was around the time our second daughter was born, and Mu Mu was an instinctive, gifted child carer. She would bathe or change the baby with an expert touch; she would gently pat her back until she fell asleep. She would play for hours with our toddler, sitting on the floor, joining her world. She may have failed her Tenth Standard, but Mu Mu taught me a lot.

She rarely referred to Saw Myo again, but I was reminded of her heartbreak each time her phone rang, programmed with the mournful ringtone that she had downloaded. 'I'm a big, big girl in a big, big world, it's not a big, big thing if you leave me,' it sang, before Mu Mu answered the call. One day, a few weeks after she had returned from the camp, I thought he had called her. Mu Mu had shut herself in the laundry room, speaking in a voice I had never heard before, agitated, a little aggressive. Then I heard her weeping.

She emerged, looking punched and red eyed.

'Was it Saw Myo?' I asked.

'No,' she said. 'My daddy.'

Mu Mu had been sending money back to her family since the day she paid off her debt to the broker. She was the family breadwinner. During her first few years in Bangkok, she barely bought anything for herself: no shampoo, no snacks, no little treats. She used the bar of cracked soap by the kitchen sink to wash her hair; she ate only the meals supplied by her employers. Her family seemed to have a lot of outgoings. First, there was her younger sister Phyu Phyu's education. A year behind Mu Mu at school, Phyu Phyu had done well in her Tenth Standard exams and became the first member of the family to go to university. When she moved to the city to study economics at Rangoon University, Mu Mu paid for everything. Then there was her older sister's wedding. Mu Mu footed the entire bill. 'I paid for the dress, the flowers, for the video, the food, everything,' she said. She couldn't attend herself, and no one sent her photographs. Mu Mu didn't mind saving for these important family expenditures, but as the years went by, the demands kept coming. 'My mother kept asking for money and I never asked what it was for. Whatever I gave them, it wasn't enough.' At times Mu Mu felt worn down by work – the ceaseless sweeping, mopping and scrubbing – and she would suggest to her parents it was time for her to come home, even for a short while. 'Sometimes I wanted to go back,' she said. 'But if I called them and suggested it they would shout at me and say, "What are you going to do here? You don't even have an education."'

Back in Hpa'an, Mu Mu's family was unravelling, but Mu Mu knew none of it. The demise of their fortunes had begun with the loss of her father's liquor job, followed by the new telephone regulations and a failed attempt to start a fish farm. The family was in debt. Nearly a year after Mu Mu's departure (when she had cleared her debts to her trafficker), the money started to arrive from Bangkok, sent through a complicated arrangement, known as *hundi*, that smoothed the flow of remittances to Burma's cash economy. Rather than paying off their creditors, Mu Mu's mother, with more money in her hands than she had held in a long time, took a gamble on the lottery. She lost and bet again, borrowing money from a friend in an attempt to recoup Mu Mu's hard-earned wages. She kept losing, but she kept betting. Each month Mu Mu's money was gambled away – some modest wins only served to fire her mother's hope that the big prize, which would solve all their problems, was just around the corner.

As the years went by, Mu Mu was able to send back more and more money. With good spoken English and her likeable manner, she had graduated from working for Thai employers to foreign expatriate families and now commanded a good salary. She was able to send hundreds of dollars home each month, way above the earning potential of any of her relatives, even her graduate sister Phyu Phyu. News from home was restricted to a monthly phone call, usually with her father, which generally focused on money – the details of how much she would send and when it would arrive. Mu Mu didn't find out about the gambling until it was already way out of hand. As the debts mushroomed, Mu Mu's parents had sold off their meagre assets: the phone line, their motorbike, a small portable stereo. It hadn't been enough. They had to get a loan from the government, a mortgage at an eye-watering interest rate. It still wasn't enough. Every day the creditors came knocking. But her desperate mother kept on betting. 'My mother was gambling four times a day. She stopped cooking at home, cleaning the house. She stopped washing herself. She got crazy. She kept losing and she wanted to win it back. She was going mad, going around all her friends and relatives asking for more loans.'

No one would lend her any more. Each day more and more people came to the house, angry, aggressive, demanding their money back. She had run out of options. One night, Mu Mu's mother skipped town. That's when her father called her, told her everything. Mu Mu was in shock. All the years of toiling, scrimping, saving and sending her wages home had come to this. She had left a poor family with a simple house, a phone line and a motorbike. She thought she could make their lives better, build the family's future. Now they owned nothing. 'We had gone backwards. I thought now I have no boyfriend, and I have no family. I felt like I was in prison.'

❧ ✿ ✿ ✿ ✿ ✿ ❧

In the 1950s, if you wanted to travel from London to the exotic yet impoverished kingdom of Thailand, you would fly first to the busy regional hub Rangoon, the city that in the early twentieth century was South-east Asia's most developed and cosmopolitan metropolis. From there you would transfer to a small propeller aircraft to fly on to Bangkok's small Don Muang airfield. How times had changed. In 2006, Thailand, by now a thriving middle-income country with an economy more than four times the size of Burma's (despite the two countries' comparable size, population and resources), opened the state-of-the-art Suvarnabhumi airport, a giant glass-and-steel edifice with one hundred and twenty departure gates, from where you could fly directly to all corners of the earth. In the same year, Burma upgraded its main airport in Rangoon, shifting passengers from a tatty old terminal which resembled a bus station in northern England, to a new, clean international terminal, with five departure gates and two baggage carousels. Burma, its isolated economy ruined by the military's disastrous experiment in socialism, had completely missed out on the meteoric growth that had flung its neighbour into a new economic age. If history had taken a different course, the migration could have been the other way round: hundreds of thousands of Thais could have been trying to sneak across the mountains to seek their fortunes in Burma. But in the early twenty-first century, that was how the arbitrage worked.

This was the backdrop to Mu Mu's young life, and I understood why she thought twice about coming with us to Rangoon. For her and her friends, the opportunities were in prospering Thailand, not in floundering Burma. Her own family's story seemed to underscore that, and I think part of her wanted to forget about them, move on. At first, Mu Mu had declined our invitation to accompany us to Rangoon. But duty to family runs deep through Burmese veins. With us, she had the opportunity to earn her Bangkok salary on the other side of the border – she could visit home, and begin sifting through the wreckage of her family's life.

With visas pasted in our passports, our family of four took a Thai Airways flight from Bangkok to Rangoon, landing in the semi-darkness of the early evening on a runway slick with monsoon rain. A few days later, Mu Mu, passportless, walked across the muddy border to the Burmese town of Myawaddy. Wasn't that dangerous? 'Going back is not a problem, it's very easy,' Mu Mu told me. 'No one is trying to go that way.'

# 3
# Burmese Shadows

A few days after our arrival in Rangoon I discovered an old business card in my purse. I thought I had purged my belongings of anything that could identify me as a journalist, and in my anxious frame of mind I ripped it up into little pieces and threw it into the waste-paper basket in the apartment that was our temporary home while we looked for somewhere to rent. It was in a serviced block, like a hotel, and maids came to the door each day to clean it. The bits of business card lay there, a jigsaw puzzle waiting to be pieced together again. Fearing one of the cleaners could be a spy, I picked up the small white pieces of card, stuffed them into an empty drinks can, swilled a bit of water around in the bottom, put it on the floor and crushed it with my foot.

We had landed in Rangoon at a time of intense paranoia and scrutiny. After its shameful handling of Nargis, the regime launched yet another crackdown on suspected dissidents. The popular comedian Zarganar was handed a forty-five-year jail term for daring to criticise the government's slow response to the cyclone. The twenty-seven-year-old rap star Zayar Thaw received a six-year sentence for belonging to the youth group Generation Wave that was formed during the Saffron Revolution. More than a hundred activists, including Buddhist monks, students and bloggers, were convicted of spurious crimes during the month we arrived in Burma, and dispatched to squalid jails across the gulag. The round-up appeared to be aimed at eliminating all opposition to the junta before national elections – the first in two decades – were held in 2010. Foreign journalists were strictly banned from reporting from Burma; those who were discovered were interrogated, deported and blacklisted. I had come to Rangoon hoping to use my status as a 'trailing spouse' as cover to continue my newspaper reporting, but, for the moment at least, it was not the time to take risks. I decided to embrace my role and discover the city just as an expatriate housewife would.

❧ ✿ ✿ ✿ ✿ ✿ ☙

My memories of Rangoon from my week reporting the uprising were limited to a few vivid snapshots of fear: my taxi careening away from me, protestors running, a strained silence in the hotel lift. I had seen only a city in trauma, now I would be able to explore it at its resting rate. Rangoon was bustling, enchanting, but having just lost its status as capital, it was a metropolis in gentle decay. On its cracked pavements, tea shop owners had arranged low wooden stools around tin tables set with rolls of rough tissue paper in plastic holders, tooth picks and bowls of sweet jaggery. Women in flowered *tamein* sarongs sat cross-legged, fanning themselves next to bubbling cauldrons of sweet corn. A cobbler with a pitch next to a thundering generator glued on a loose sole; a young woman in charge of two push-button landline phones on a trestle table rested her head on her open palm, barely acknowledging customers who handed her a twenty kyat note for each call.

The port city of Rangoon became Burma's capital in 1885, when the British completed their conquest of the north. The colonial masters built the city to a grid plan, with the streets running up from the Rangoon River identified by ascending number and the cross streets named after British colonial statesmen (Phayre, Dalhousie, Fraser), and since renamed to recall the great Burmese king Anawrahta, the nineteenth-century resistance fighter Mahabandoola, and independence hero Aung San. The British left in 1948, bequeathing a messy political legacy but also an array of grand buildings that survive to this day – a remarkable, living colonial film set. From pavements spattered with the red spit of betel-nut chewers, I looked up at pale green Victorian-era tenements, flowers of mildew staining the peeling paintwork, with shuttered windows, filigree balconies and steep wooden stairs. Around the corner were sturdy red-brick buildings reminiscent of Manchester or Sheffield, and white, neoclassical edifices that once housed thriving colonial enterprises.

In air thick with diesel fumes from decrepit Japanese cars, it was a challenge to imagine Rangoon as it had been a century ago, when the city boomed on exports of rice and timber and its infrastructure and municipal services were considered to be on a par with London. Then, the immaculate shop floors of the Rowe & Co. department store, one of the largest and most stylish emporiums in pre-war Asia, were brightly lit and replete with European fashions, homewares and familiar comforts for homesick British colonialists. Consulting my map, I located the building a block east of City Hall. Its grand entrance was boarded up, its windows were smashed and its listing wrought-iron portico sheltered stalls selling tangerines and pirated DVDs, and a tailor with a foot-powered Singer sewing machine. A little further north, the turreted red-brick Secretariat – scene of the assassination of General Aung San, father of the opposition leader Aung San Suu Kyi – was fenced off and used as a barracks for a large city centre presence of police. A few streets away, the imposing police headquarters, with its two-storey Corinthian columns, was home to more battalions of officers, its grand rooms used as dormitories or makeshift kitchens, while washing lines for navy police uniforms were strung up along its carefully proportioned balconies looking out to the Rangoon River.

A walk around almost any part of the city seemed to be rewarded with the discovery of a new treasure. Hidden behind a tangle of trees and creepers on a busy thoroughfare in the diplomatic quarter was the teak-walled Pegu Club, where British imperial officers had smoked cigars and played billiards, and whose eponymous cocktail – a mix of gin, lime juice, orange curaçao and bitters – is still served in plush hotels the world over. I had wanted to find it, imagining that my great-uncle Douglas had drunk at its bar before fleeing the Japanese invasion of the Second World War. I approached warily, under the watch of security guards employed by the Russian embassy next door. One of them came towards me, and I expected to be shooed off. But in fact he wanted to be my tour guide, and, accompanied by a pair of curious dogs, led me to the front of the building to open a creaking, unlocked door. A layer of dust and rat droppings covered the parquet floor, but the Pegu Club's magnificent teak bar, sweeping staircases and original black Bakelite light switches were still in place.

The survival of Rangoon's colonial buildings, albeit in assorted states of decay, owed more to Burma's retarded development than to a strong will to preserve these architectural gems. In 1962, the military junta seized power and began to cut Burma off from the world. Over half a century, the isolationist policies of Burma's reclusive generals throttled foreign business dealings and provoked American and European sanctions. While cities such as Bangkok, Shanghai and Manila underwent frenzies of development, sprouting skyscrapers from every square foot of land, Rangoon's city centre remained remarkably untouched. In

2005, reportedly on the advice of astrologers, the military government abruptly relocated the capital to Naypyidaw, a newly constructed city two hundred miles north in Burma's central scrublands. Rangoon was left as a mouldering testament to another era.

One afternoon, I took the ferry across the Rangoon River to the suburb of Dala, just a ten-minute ride over grey waters but a world away from the faded grandeur of Strand Road on the city side. Clustered around the ferry pontoon was a small village of wooden houses, still under repair after the cyclone, as well as teashops, a hair salon and some small clothes shops. The village was built around a lattice of narrow concrete lanes, just wide enough for a pedicab. A short walk took me quickly into flat, open countryside. I hired a motorbike taxi (permitted only on this side of the river) and we headed east. There were fields of wheat and maize, dissected by irrigation channels and dotted with little bamboo houses. On a raised dyke between the fields, I saw a father and his daughter, perhaps three years old, making fuel pats out of cow dung. We rode out to a riverfront village half an hour away, downstream of the city. Wooden fishing canoes were lined up on the shore and in the water were the brick mounds of old jetties, a monument to healthier economic times, but long since collapsed. The village was poor. Wooden houses were raised up on stilts from the boggy ground, the balconies at the back of each home not for relaxing but for keeping pigs. It was late in the afternoon and children were everywhere, running between houses, sitting on benches watching adults playing billiards around a large, tarpaulin-sheltered table. On the step of one house was a pile of little flip-flops and tattered shoes. Through the doorway I could see school textbooks open on the floor, and children working with their pencils.

≈ ✿ ✿ ✿ ✿ ✿ ≈

If Rangoon's physical landscape was easy enough to navigate, its human terrain was not. Save for a brief interaction with a second-hand bookstall owner, estate agent or taxi driver, my conversations with Burmese people were scarce and insubstantial. Few people were comfortable talking openly to a foreigner; such conversations would attract the unwanted attention of the authorities. There were smiles and stares, but apart from street children selling postcards, people kept their distance. After the dramas of the past months, the city seemed to be keeping its collective head down, staying out of trouble. There was a Burmese phrase, which I would later learn, '*ma lou*', *ma shou*', *ma pyou*' – 'Don't do anything, things won't get messed up, you won't get fired'. It applied specifically to the workplace, but its sense of purposeful passivity seemed to sum up Rangoon's prevailing mood.

We found a house to rent near both the international school and the Australian embassy in Golden Valley, a well-to-do district of substantial houses set in generous tropical gardens near Inya Lake. From the first-floor balcony there was a view across the rooftops to the golden, bell-shaped stupa that dominated the city's low-rise skyline. Our landlord, a retired sea captain, had shown us around our new home with an air of melancholy, while his wife waited patiently in the passenger seat of their small saloon car. The whitewash of the 1970s-built house was bruised purple and green from the lashings of monsoon torrents. The concrete driveway was cracked and coated in slimy green moss. A broken drainpipe hung limply down the side of one wall. But it was the garden that was the most convincing witness to the elemental drubbing that Rangoon had recently endured. At intervals around its perimeter were wooden stumps, marking the graves of once shady trees that had been toppled by the cyclone. With the greenery shorn away, we were left with the tender sight of barbed wire looped along the top of the garden wall, and a view of our neighbour's water tanks and outhouses. Once Rangoon's residents had absorbed the shock of the cyclone – the loss of life and the damage to their homes – they had turned their attention to another casualty of the storm: thousands of the city's trees. 'It is a great pain for us, a great tragedy,' our landlord said softly as we paced around the garden, examining the messy tangle of plants and shrubs that remained. The destruction of so many of Rangoon's venerable old banyans, mahoganies and rain trees had stripped away its charming, leafy canopy, leaving the hardscrabble city beneath painfully exposed to the sun's glare.

As required, we registered with the neighbourhood State Peace and Development Council, where the flag of the Republic of the Union of Myanmar (soon to change to a new design in an overnight directive from the junta) hung on a pole outside. The authorities kept a list of all the residents in each house, including children, complete with ID or passport details. No one else was permitted to stay in our home; any overnight guests would need to register their names with the local SPDC office. The household lists were part of a pervasive system of control that reached from the top of government all the way down to the home. The regime's secret police units were used to intimidate the civilian population and monitor people's movements, keeping a particular eye on potential dissidents such as community workers, journalists and artists. Phone lines were tapped, foreign embassies were bugged and even the military government's own officials spied upon. At a local level, each SPDC office had an intelligence agent assigned who oversaw a network of informers, ideally recruiting at least one per street. On the phone, on the bus, in the teashop, people were always careful; they never knew who was listening in.

But Burma was a country of contradictions. Despite the bureaucracy, the Orwellian surveillance, to an outsider Rangoon could feel like a surprisingly hospitable place. The expatriate community was small and close knit; my daughter got a place in the nursery of a thriving international school and soon began rehearsing for the Christmas nativity play; I arranged swimming lessons for her with a gentle, elderly man who had once represented Burma at the Olympics. If ever we missed soft cheese, Italian ham or French wine there was a deli to cater to our needs. There were parties, film festivals and tennis matches on shaded courts by the lake. This privileged scene was the preserve of foreigners and a small group of wealthy, middle-class Burmese, however. I found it hard to get a sense of the lives of more typical Rangoon residents: the man at the junction on Dhammazedi Road who sold strings of jasmine flowers for five cents apiece; the armed policemen who manned the sandbagged position at the foot of our lane; the women who wandered the neighbourhood selling winter strawberries in little woven bamboo boxes. It was dangerous to initiate conversations, to ask questions, and my early impressions of Burmese life were restricted to casual observations and happenstance.

One day, two uniformed soldiers and another man came up the track to our house and rang the little brass bell that was tied with wire to the gate. I opened it, and they took two steps inside. They stood in a stiff row, eyes to the ground, the two soldiers flanking the civilian, a bookseller. He carried a sling bag containing a dozen or so Burmese paperback books, novels and recipe books. He showed me a couple of them with trembling, tattooed hands. 'Buy, buy!' said one of the soldiers, his voice low but with an urgency in his command. The men had the searching eyes and hollowed-out cheeks of hunger. The soldier pointed to the badge on the arm of his green army uniform, pulling the sleeve. Wordlessly, he was saying: 'We are soldiers, you have to buy.' His colleague, who spoke a little English, tugged at his empty breast pocket. 'No money, no food,' he said. I went into the house to fetch them each a thousand kyat note. Under the watch of next-door's gardener, who had climbed his ladder to look over the wall, I walked slowly back and handed over the money. The soldiers straightened their backs, clicked their heels and saluted.

⁂ ✿ ✿ ✿ ✿ ✿ ✿ ⁂

It was the National Day public holiday, with a high sky of wispy clouds and tolerable temperatures under thirty-five degrees. A month since the end of the rains, a touch of moisture still lingered in the air. Driving my husband's white station wagon, with the logo of his NGO emblazoned on the side, I was on my way to the hair salon, where my humidity-wrecked hair would be tamed and smoothed for just a few dollars.

I drove down the stony track that led from our house, turned right at the small, family-run shop that sold handmade cotton dresses, past the newly built, ostentatious mansion named Paradise where water flowed in silent, flat panels over its granite surrounding wall, then alongside the wooden kiosks selling instant noodles, bananas and cigarettes, to the shady junction where the trishaw drivers snoozed under the outstretched arms of a banyan tree. I indicated left on the main road and drove by Bahan High School No. 2, deserted for the holiday, the national flag hoisted on a pole in the playground. My route took me down Shwegondine Road, past what had been pointed out to me as the headquarters of Aung San Suu Kyi's National League for Democracy party, housed in a rundown terrace between two furniture shops. After years of harassment, and with hundreds of its members, including Suu Kyi, imprisoned, the party rarely held meetings and its offices were usually padlocked and deserted. But today a crowd of people was gathered outside, men and women wearing red armbands, most with heads bowed, looking uncomfortable, frightened even. It was the first gathering of any kind I had seen in Rangoon. I parked the car and walked towards it.

I was approached by a benevolent-looking man with opaque, pale brown eyes and neatly combed grey hair. He introduced himself as U Hla Thein, a member of parliament (I was confused, surely there was no parliament?), and steered me through the overspill of NLD supporters on the pavement. The crowd of about seventy was mostly quiet; their very presence, in front of the plain-clothed military intelligence officers across the street, was their statement, and a stunningly brave one. 'Aren't you scared?' I asked U Hla Thein. 'No,' he said with a smile. 'We don't care.' Inside the gloomy shophouse, with its damp, peeling walls, it was hard to believe I was in the offices of a political party that could, or should, have been running a country of more than fifty million people.

In May 1990, when Aung San Suu Kyi was already in detention at her home, Burma held its first general elections for thirty years. No one was sure what the ruling State Law and Order Restoration Council (SLORC) was expecting, but it seemed the governing generals believed that even after all these years of slow degradation, the people of Burma, subservient for so long, would duly vote in the military's proxy party. That wasn't what happened. Suu Kyi's NLD won the election by a landslide, and the junta, shocked, simply refused to cede power. Parliament was never convened, but candidates like U Hla Thein, elected in their constituencies, continued to introduce themselves as MPs, as he did to me, more than eighteen years later.

We tried to squeeze forward through the mass of bodies. 'Are you a diplomat?' someone asked. 'Er, yes,' I replied. I was ushered to a plastic chair near the front.

Sitting in front of the NLD central executive committee, comprised mostly of elderly men, I was now stingingly self-conscious, worried about my opportunistic fib and also what I was wearing – a sleeveless top and flimsy, almost see-through skirt, certainly not diplomat's attire. Worse still, there were several enthusiastic photographers pacing around snapping everything – were they NLD activists, from the media or even intelligence agents? To be photographed in this pariah place would be a nightmare. I crossed my legs and hunched over with my elbow on my knee and my hand shielding my eyes, as if trying to block out the glaring sun.

The speeches had already begun. U Hla Pe, a member of the executive committee, read dryly from a written speech calling for political prisoners to be released and for the junta to review a new constitution which enshrined the military's role in any future elected government. A woman in the audience, her greying hair pinned back, wiped away silent tears as she listened to demands she probably believed would never be met. U Hla Pe finished, took a sip from his water glass, his hand shaking, and was helped down from the wooden podium. He rejoined the NLD top brass seated behind him; two rows of noble, old men, their political dreams reduced to empty protocol. Most of the party's best political minds were behind bars. Communication with their leader Suu Kyi was impossible. 'We don't speak to her, we don't hear from her, no no no,' said U Hla Thein, who had taken the seat next to me. 'How can we know what she's thinking?' Rudderless and reduced by imprisonments, the remnants of the party were trying to decide whether to contest elections set for 2010, the first to be held since 1990. There was little prospect of a fair vote; everyone expected Burma's generals would ensure that their puppet party, the Union Solidarity and Development Party (USDP), would be the winner. Western diplomats had met privately with NLD leaders to urge them to participate in the vote, warning them that the party risked sinking into irrelevance otherwise. But party members had their doubts. 'In the West you always talk of a level-playing field,' another disenfranchised MP told me. 'Here our game is played on the side of a mountain.' He asked my nationality and thanked me for coming. I felt like a fraud, but I didn't trust even this man enough to confess that I was a journalist.

The meeting over, there were hugs and laughter and news shared among comrades who saw each other all too rarely. They streamed out, the men holding hands or linking fingers in that comfortable, unconscious gesture that is the preserve of Asian males. They made their way down to the bus stops at Shwegondine junction, with wary sideways glances at the spies across the street.

I weaved through the crowd and crossed the road to my car parked in a small lot on the other side. Beneath the pavement of cracked concrete blocks, a trickling sewer exhaled its fetid gases. While focusing on each careful step, I became aware that someone was following me. I swung round to see a man in a white shirt and *longyi,* his hair slicked down with oil. It is hard to describe, but regime people had a certain look – swarthy and sullen. They carried satchels for their notebooks. Instead of going straight to the car, with its NGO logo, I walked fast to the Yuzana Hotel, and straight to the hair salon, now an hour late for my appointment. Lying on a cushioned bed with my hair in the sink, next to a backlit mural of an Alpine mountain and sparkling stream, I surrendered to a head massage, turning over what I had seen in the NLD office. Basins of warm water were poured over my hair and my head was gently wrapped in a towel. The image of the man who followed me was fading from my mind, I was thinking about everything else, the privilege of witnessing this extraordinary meeting. By the time my hair had been dried, I had almost forgotten him.

I stepped through the frosted glass door and stopped still. Across the lobby, sitting on a couch, there he was again, a newspaper in hand. Or was it him? I wasn't completely sure. I couldn't look again, and I couldn't turn around as I walked fast, head down, towards the car, parked between the hotel and the NLD building. Horribly aware of the aid agency's name clearly painted on both sides of the car, I quickly got in, and immediately wished I hadn't. I could have got a taxi, or walked in the other direction towards the pagoda or a shopping centre, found a group to get lost in. But it was too late. I slammed the door and bumped on to the road, hitting the passenger side on the kerb. I accelerated into the middle lane and indicated right at the empty school. I checked my rear-view mirror and saw there were no cars preparing to turn with me. I breathed out. No tail, I thought. It was only as I pulled the steering wheel down that I spotted the motorbike.

In contrast to other Asian cities, motorcycles were rare in Rangoon. They were banned purportedly for reasons of safety but in fact as a means of control. New cars were the preserve of the very rich, thanks to a massive import duty, and the streets were choked with ancient jalopies coughing out lead-filled exhaust fumes. But even those were unaffordable to most: my taxi driver's rented car, for example, a 1983 Toyota Sprinter, had a resale value of $27,000. Bicycles too were banned from the main thoroughfares and so every day Rangoonites packed themselves on to decrepit buses. That way, the junta reasoned, mass movement in the city was fully controlled – a flash demonstration would be impossible to organise. So the motorbike I saw in the mirror could mean only one thing: special branch.

I kept driving towards home, checking my mirror as the bike followed me at each turn. I couldn't lead him to my house, with our names registered at the neighbourhood SPDC office – that would make us instantly identifiable, as if the NGO logo wasn't enough. Panicked, I drove to a small bakery tucked up a lane close to our house, parked and went inside the shop. It wasn't a very good manoeuvre; I had taken myself into a dead end. In fact, it was laughably bad. I waited as long as I could, examining the different breads and imported jams and homemade cheeses. When I ran out of time to be plausibly selecting a loaf of bread, I drove out again, expecting to see the motorbike at the end of the driveway, but he was gone. I suppose an address in his notebook was all he needed to feel his work was done. The thing I discovered about the special branch agents was that although as a whole they were dangerous, individually they seemed rather ineffectual, buzzing around town on their orange motorbikes with helmets askew.

✢ ✿ ✿ ✿ ✿ ✿ ✢

'You did what?' my husband Dan shouted, furious at my stupidity. And now it did seem really stupid. As enthralled as I had been by this rare glimpse of the opposition's clandestine world, my actions now had the potential to cause a lot of trouble. It was a deeply sensitive time for aid agencies in Burma. In the aftermath of the cyclone international organisations were trying to scale up their operations, a process that involved painstaking negotiations with government ministries mistrustful of foreign organisations. International NGOs like my husband's had worked hard to cultivate an apolitical stance in order to get aid through to the hundreds of thousands of people in dire need. Visiting the offices of the outlawed NLD was not something their staff should be seen to be doing.

Shaken up, and keen to get out of the house, I remembered I was due at the Girls' Tea Party, an annual expatriate fundraising event in Golden Valley, just half a mile or so from where the NLD meeting had taken place. The women-only sale of rather pricey, pretty purses, table mats, scented candles, jewellery and other nick-nacks, with sparkling white wine for refreshment, was laid out on trestle tables on the rolling lawn of a wooden colonial villa, home to a French-American family. The trees were festooned with lanterns and strings of fairy lights and the family's multitude of pet rabbits hopped around the grass. This was another side to Rangoon, carefree and frivolous. It was little more than an hour since my brush with a special branch agent. Now I was back in familiar territory, but felt strangely removed. I hurried up the driveway, grabbed my flute of prosecco, and gratefully fell into conversation with some friends.

# 4
# The Fixer

'**D**id you know that we are all addicted to gambling?' Zayar asked cheerfully. The young reporter and I were discussing ideas for a newspaper piece. I recalled Mu Mu's story, and the damage gambling had wrought on her family. In my neighbourhood in Rangoon, I had seen hand-pushed lottery carts, blaring loud, perky music in an effort to entice people out of their homes to buy tickets. The lottery was run by the government, and didn't seem to get anyone too excited. 'No, that's not it, this isn't the government's thing, it's run by the people,' Zayar said. 'Tomorrow I can show you.'

＊＊＊＊＊

By 10 a.m. it was getting hot, even in the shade of the colonial apartment blocks along Mahabandoola Street. Stepping around the little plastic stools that encircled the pop-up eateries selling fried rice pancakes, Zayar and I walked down to the busy bus stop at the end of Bogolay Zay Street. The buses wheezed up, their tattooed conductors hanging out of the side doors clutching dirty wads of twenty kyat notes, shouting out their destinations. Unadventurous as this may sound, I was about to take my first trip on a Burmese bus. Up to then, I had not thought of Rangoon buses as a potential means of transport. A Burmese woman friend of mine, who worked in a city centre office, had told me that her forty-minute morning and evening bus commutes were the worst part of her day. Aggressive conductors packed the buses as full as possible, and she would invariably find herself standing, wedged in, and at the mercy of belchers and gropers. The city's ancient bus fleet included snub-nosed, Second World War-era models, which we expatriates considered quaint, and would buy painted wooden replicas of them as souvenirs. But jumping aboard one of those heaving, suffocatingly hot and possibly dangerous wrecks was another matter. In truth, with buses so packed and intimidating and the city's taxis plentiful and cheap, the only foreigners you would see braving Rangoon's public transport were a few hardened backpackers.

We boarded a number 43 bus. Travelling against the rush-hour traffic, we managed to find space on a wooden bench. As a foreigner I attracted curious looks, not at all hostile, and plenty of shy smiles. I smiled back, chatted to Zayar, and enjoyed Rangoon's eclectic cityscape from the bus window. A wonky wooden house with stained-glass windows and elaborate cupolas nestled in the shade of tamarind trees. An unexplained patch of waste ground was strewn with twisted plastic bags. A jarring new apartment building of smoked glass and metalwork painted in primary colours bore the sign 'Motherland'. I tried to convince myself that our cover story – that I was an English teacher with a fascination for the Burmese way of life, such a fascination that I was driven to take notes and even record conversations on my tape recorder – was actually credible.

At a stop on a busy highway we got off and walked single-file along the verge for a hundred yards before turning into the narrow streets of Daubon Township. Daubon was a shabby neighbourhood of wooden or simple brick houses built along a grid of roads just wide enough to take a car but used mostly by pedestrians and bicycles. Some of the streets had been paved with big concrete blocks; others were simply compacted earth that turned into rivers of mud during the monsoon. Banyan and banana trees lent charm to the down-at-heel suburb and at the centre was an airy Buddhist monastery with a sparkly gold arched entrance and a weed-coated pond buzzing with mosquitoes. We ambled along the walkways, past hungry dogs and toddlers with dirty vests and bare bottoms and a woman bathing with two buckets of water in her front yard, maintaining her modesty with a cotton *longyi* which clung to her wet body as she scrubbed her arms and neck.

We came to a wooden shack called the Sky Café and took a table under the green tarpaulin awning. Old women smoking cheroots, young mechanics with oil-stained hands and women breastfeeding their babies drifted in and sat down on low plastic chairs. Like everyone else, we ordered the strong, sweet tea served in small glasses with an inch of condensed milk that sinks to the bottom. As the clock ticked up towards midday, the waiter revved up the generator to power the big TV that was hooked up to a satellite dish on the roof. The café's patrons shuffled in their seats, stretched their necks, made sure they had a view of the screen. This was what Zayar had brought me to see. In an atmosphere of mounting anticipation, the crowd of labourers, hawkers and housewives was waiting not for a football or horse-racing result, but for the price of the Bangkok Stock Exchange index at its lunchtime close. These were people who had never owned shares in anything – their interest was not in the performance of the stock market, but in the random, final two digits of the share price, on which most had bet at least half of their daily wage.

On came the cinematic theme music for the noon newscast on Thai Channel 9, and two elegantly coiffed presenters, a man and a woman, smiled at us from the television screen. The pristine environment of the news studio – the male presenter's starched white cuffs, the woman's glossy pink lips and the glinting diamond at her throat – seemed at odds with our own grungy surroundings. No one in the Sky Café understood the newsreaders' warbling Thai vowels, but no one was interested. Their eyes were fixed on the ticker scrolling along the bottom of the screen, showing us first the temperature in Bangkok, then the baht exchange rate and then, yes, the stock index price, and most importantly, those last two digits after the decimal point. After a moment of straight-backed hope, all eyes on the screen, the crowd slumped. A short silence marked their disappointment, and the hubbub of chat resumed.

❧ ✿ ✿ ✿ ✿ ✿ ❧

In 2009, Burma was a country with no political freedom, few economic choices and little hope. In the crowded townships of Rangoon, in declining market towns and impoverished rural villages, everyone, it seemed, was trying to bet their way out of a miserable existence. That afternoon, Zayar took me to meet Kyaw Kyaw, (pronounced Jaw Jaw), who worked for his family business in Daubon, repairing motors and generators on the ground floor of their house. For him, betting was something to look forward to. 'Twice a day, I am happy. I have hope,' he said, trying to explain why it was worth losing so much of his meagre income. 'If you are on your way to the market with 1,000 kyats (one dollar) in your pocket, you think you are a poor man. You can't buy much. But if you spend it on a lottery ticket, you have bought the chance to be rich.'

Kyaw Kyaw, thirty-five and single, gambled on the 'two digits' lottery both lunchtime and evening, giving a dollar each time to the saleswomen who go door to door taking bets. Those women took a 10 per cent cut and handed over the bets to the bigger bookmakers. Like all of Burma's small-time gamblers, Kyaw Kyaw lost nearly every day. But the wins were what he remembered. 'When I win I'll go out and buy lots of food, we'll cook for my family and friends. It's like a party every time,' he said.

I was sitting on the lino floor of Kyaw Kyaw's house, with its aroma of engine oil and curry spices, my notebook back in use after several redundant months, just talking to people. My legs were folded beneath me and I could feel the sweat behind my knees. Kyaw Kyaw's eighty-one-year-old grandfather was sitting cross-legged by my shoulder, on a wooden bed base with a woven bamboo mat on top. He was silent but seemingly content to be in the company of the busy workshop, and I was happy to be in someone else's house on the other side of Rangoon, away from my limited expat world.

As Kyaw Kyaw's mother crouched down to place the tea tray between us on the floor, a middle-aged man sauntered in through the open front door. He had the self-possessed look of someone I identified as a regime spy. He was head of the neighbourhood State Peace and Development Council and word had reached him that a foreign woman was around, asking questions. There were tense smiles and handshakes and offers of tea. Zayar explained that I was a teacher, newly arrived in Rangoon. They chatted a little in Burmese. 'Where's she from?' the official asked. 'Manchester,' replied Zayar (this we had established during our chat the day before). The name of my native city prompted the customary response and the official began to list Manchester United players – *Rooney, Scholes, Giggs*. With a tense smile, Zayar encouraged him, trying to lighten the atmosphere. When the agent asked for our names, Zayar confidently wrote down his details on a piece of paper. He handed it to me. I was panicking, I was about to use my writer's pseudonym, but that still seemed too close to the real me. Somehow I became Sarah Irish (maybe the Irish bit would confuse them?) and wrote my correct address with the wrong house number, frightened that an attempt at a complete fabrication would expose me as a fraud. Apparently satisfied, the SPDC agent folded the paper into his shirt pocket and left.

'Did you give him your real name?' I asked Zayar.

'Of course not,' he said. 'It's no problem.'

❧ ✿ ✿ ✿ ✿ ✿ ❧

The kind of unsophisticated subterfuge I used with Zayar could only get me so far; chats in teashops, markets and taxis were never going to generate any real scoops. Sometimes I got lucky. One morning, after dropping off my daughter at nursery, I went to use the Wi-Fi in the marble-floored lobby of the Summit Parkview Hotel. The comfortable couches were usually occupied with tourists, the occasional businessman and wealthy Burmese for whom the hotel was a popular venue for weddings and parties. I sat down and opened my laptop to send some emails, but found myself tuning into a conversation led by a smart Burmese woman with Gucci glasses and a YSL bag perched on the next sofa. Speaking in English, she was delivering a pushy sales patter. She was clearly confident about what she was selling, but it took me a while to work out what it actually was. Slowly it dawned on me: her product was people. 'We supply only strong bodies,' she said crisply. 'That is our guarantee.'

I tried not to look at her, and strained to hear above the tinkling of a wooden xylophone being played by a man in traditional Burmese dress. I started to take notes on my computer. The woman was a supplier of workers for deep-sea trawlers, and her stock of men came from Burma's beautiful but impoverished Inle Lake, where fishing the tranquil waters no longer made enough to feed a family. 'These are just simple fishermen; they are not educated, but what we promise you is strong bodies,' she said, using a phrase she repeated again and again.

Her potential customers were middlemen, probably Chinese. Through a translator, they discussed placing the men on boats in the South China Sea, trawling for tuna. With the aid of pictures on her laptop, she described a selection process worthy of a livestock market.

'We make them stand in the sun for one hour,' the woman said. 'In the middle of the day when it is very hot. We see how they manage, if they look uncomfortable.'

The group leaned in to view the photographs on her computer. 'We make them carry twenty kilos, like this,' she continued, showing them pictures I could not see. The middlemen sucked on 555 cigarettes. 'For deep-sea fishing, they may need to carry very big fish for long distances across the ship.' Then came the seasickness test. 'We put them in here,' the woman said. I couldn't see the picture, but I thought it must have been an enclosed truck or some sort of container on water. 'Then we start to move them around. If they are sick or find it hard to breathe we don't select them. This is how we select the best bodies.' She looked expectantly at her potential clients who lit more cigarettes and began to discuss the price.

This depressing insight was certainly a story for me, but so many questions were left frustratingly unanswered because of my fear of being exposed as a journalist. Real journalism depends on asking questions, demanding answers, building sources, door-stepping officials and holding those with power to account. I could do none of that. Foreign reporters caught at it were unceremoniously deported – I had seen many examples – and others who came and left undetected were swiftly blacklisted once their articles were published.

With no Internet access at home I moved around Internet cafés and used the Wi-Fi in hotel lobbies to write and file my stories. My articles were published under my pseudonym, of course, but I was always anxious about who was watching me, who knew what was on the screen of my computer. I opened new email accounts in different names, all with different passwords, which I tried to commit to memory. Some of them I forgot. I liked to think that if I couldn't get into my accounts, the Military Intelligence agents couldn't either. Reporting was never easy, but the frustrations were far greater for Burmese journalists. This was their story, but they were not allowed to tell it properly.

❧ ✿ ✿ ✿ ✿ ✿ ☙

Zayar's first job in journalism, at *Modern Weekly*, came with a salary of thirty dollars a month. There were only a few computers in the office and he would have to wait his turn to use one, often writing out his articles by hand. The power supply was intermittent, and when it was off, he would have to contend with the noise and heat of the generator thundering away outside the door. The journalists had no budget for reporting stories; they got around the city on foot or by bus and used a notepad and pencil rather than a tape recorder. Only the editor had a mobile phone, and permission was needed even to make a call from the office landline.

Once their articles were written, the next stop was the censor. Since the 1962 military coup, all parts of the Burmese media had been strictly controlled. Newspapers and TV broadcasts, songs, poetry and films were censored to filter out any criticism of the government, or indeed any bad news about Burma. Journalists had to submit every newspaper article, TV and radio script to the Press Scrutiny Board. The board's favourite stories included reports on the daily activities of Burma's senior generals – opening a new bridge, for example, or dishing out helpful advice to rice farmers. Anything perceived as even mildly critical of the military regime was excised with a red pen. Big chunks of text were expurgated, rendering the rest of the article nonsensical. Often entire articles, books or poems were banned. News of the president was moved to the front page; anything negative – even stories about crime or a bad harvest – was deleted or shortened and relegated to an inside page. The country's old name of Burma was always substituted with the new, official name: Myanmar. Journalists complained that even the news articles that survived the censor would take so long to make their way through the arcane system of the censorship board that they were out of date by the time they reached the reader.

The only alternative to this numbing censorship was a highly risky one. Since the advent of military rule, international media organisations had started broadcasting into Burma from overseas, using reports smuggled out to them by clandestine reporters. Most of the contributors to the so-called exile media were already journalists working for the Burmese press. They kept their activities top secret, even among their most trusted colleagues. The price they would pay for getting caught was certain imprisonment.

The BBC and Voice of America both broadcast into the country with their Burmese language services. Standing on the fourth-floor balcony of a friend's downtown apartment one evening, we looked across the street to the open, lit windows of the colonial tenements opposite. A spider's web of wires radiated from the Internet café on the ground floor, leasing bandwidth to the apartments within reach. At 7 p.m. the familiar theme tunes of the dissident news broadcasts struck up from across the street and above and below us, as families unfurled plastic mats on the floor and set out dishes of curry, rice and clear, sour soup for dinner. This was how the Burmese people got the real news.

The Democratic Voice of Burma, or DVB, was started in 1992 as a shortwave radio station. It was hosted by the Norwegian government, and I sometimes wondered how the small group of committed, exiled Burmese editors who ran the station from Oslo had adjusted to the crisp cold of their new Scandinavian habitat. In 2005, DVB moved into video transmission, relying on the growing number of satellite dishes in Burma that received foreign television broadcasts. By that time there were estimated to be around 1.5 million satellite receivers in Burma, and given that one dish, such as the one at Sky Café, might serve several dozen people, that promised fairly good coverage among a population of more than fifty million.

DVB's work depended on a secret network of journalists inside Burma who would gather stories and smuggle out footage either on thumb drives or discs, or more riskily via the Internet, for the news to be beamed back from Oslo in a daily, two-hour package of current affairs programmes and documentaries. The technologically backward regime seemed to find it impossible to block these broadcasts. One muggy evening, on the terrace of a smart café next to Bogyoke Aung San Market, I met Thida, a DVB 'VJ' or video journalist. I should have felt a bond with this woman, a fellow undercover journalist. But as she explained her work, I realised that our professional lives had little in common. My journalistic forays were sporadic; sometimes weeks would go by without me reporting a thing. I took on jobs writing and editing reports for the United Nations and international NGOs. While these dormant periods in my journalistic life were certainly good for my cover, they also showed that I had nothing like the same commitment – and took nothing like the same risks – as some of the brave Burmese journalists I met.

Twenty-eight-year-old Thida wouldn't tell me her real name, which wasn't surprising given that two of her colleagues had recently been arrested. With her precious hand-held video camera in a patent leather bag, Thida darted around the country, gathering footage and interviews to send back to Oslo. Sometimes, she tried to pass herself off as a businesswoman or tourist, filming in secret. Sometimes, with people she felt she could trust, she told the truth.

'It's dangerous for them as well as for me,' Thida said. 'People are scared of getting into trouble. So I film them from behind, or just a silhouette, so they know they won't be identified.' She risked arrest at any time. 'Last week, I was carrying my camera and some soldiers came towards me. I panicked, and dumped my camera under a bush. Many times I've had to do that sort of thing,' she said.

DVB's video journalists made their name during the 2007 uprising. Their work filming the demonstrations by Buddhist monks and the army's violent crackdown was made famous by the Oscar-nominated feature film *Burma VJ*, and gave the regime its worst publicity for decades. To prevent the same thing happening again, the authorities passed a new law banning filming without government permission, and those who defied it and were caught were locked up for long terms. One of the cameramen who shot the film, known publicly as 'T', had been arrested in a Rangoon Internet café a few months earlier. A military court had just sentenced him to thirteen years in prison for violating Burma's Electronics Act and working illegally for a foreign media organisation. Another of Thida's colleagues, twenty-five-year-old camerawoman Hla Hla Win, had been sentenced to twenty years for transmitting news critical of the government. According to the Burma Media Association, which was based in neighbouring Thailand, at least fourteen reporters were arrested in Burma in 2009.

Like all of the Burmese dissidents I met during that time, Thida was completely single-minded. There was no room left for anything else in her life. 'My mother wants me to stop this job,' she told me. 'But I am a journalist and I love journalism. I want to get my stories out.'

The exiled media was gearing up for the 2010 elections, the first to be held in Burma since the 1990 poll that Aung San Suu Kyi's National League for Democracy had won by a landslide, but the outcome of which the junta had ignored. The elections promised a new parliament, and a government run by civilians. It was the role of DVB and other news organisations to inject a dose of realism: in the 2008 constitution, the military had put in place strong safeguards to protect their power, including reserving one quarter of seats in the two houses of parliament for military appointees. Many of those running for seats as civilians would simply hang up their army uniforms, political observers said. The NLD had dismissed the constitution as illegitimate and had decided to boycott the vote. No one was expecting much to change.

Thida left abruptly to catch an overnight bus to Mandalay. I put away my notebook and looked across the table at Zayar, who had set up the interview and had come to translate for me. He sipped on a soda with mint leaves and ice. Two elaborate Burmese puppets, with white porcelain faces and red painted lips, were strung up on either side of the café door, staring at us. From the far side of the wooden balustrade that marked off the terrace, street children selling out-of-date copies of *Time* magazine and the *International Herald Tribune* were trying to attract our attention. I wondered whether Zayar also smuggled out his reports. It was a fair bet that he did, but at that point he didn't want to talk about it.

# 5

# The King's Grandson

Getting accustomed to the hotel bicycle, I gently freewheeled down the gravelly driveway, admiring the hollyhocks and gladioli that bordered the sweeping front lawn. Between the two stone gateposts at the foot of the hill, I came to a squeaky halt, wobbled slightly and planted a foot on the ground to check for traffic. I pedalled off slowly to the right, trying to operate the seized-up gears. A gentle breeze ruffled the waters of the ornamental lake on my left, and beyond that, a line of Japanese red maples and mulberry trees rustled on the edge of the botanical gardens. The stacked roofs of a wooden, Chinese-style pagoda peeked out above the treetops. The air smelt earthy and fresh. It was the first of several occasions during my short stay in Maymyo that I would have to remind myself that I was still in Burma.

Since arriving in Rangoon – a port city that for nine months of the year is insufferably hot and wet or insufferably hot and dry – I had been tempted to visit Maymyo, the hill-station built by British colonialists to escape the fiercest of the summer months. From March to May, British officers, civil servants and their wives would decamp en masse from Rangoon to take up residence in the small town, laid out in the manner of a Surrey village, with mock-Tudor houses and pretty stone cottages. Sitting 3,500 feet above the city of Mandalay, it was comfortable and breezy, and surrounded by fields of flowers, coffee bushes and strawberries. It all sounded very enticing, but until the hot season of 2010 I hadn't found the excuse to visit.

A few weeks earlier, while on a visa-run to Bangkok (a manoeuvre that involved skipping out of the country for a few days), I had been sitting with the Burmese historian Thant Myint-U over Starbucks iced lattes in a glass-walled shopping mall. The grandson of 1960s UN Secretary-General U Thant, the younger Thant was also a former UN diplomat as well as a historian and author. He knew Burma intimately, but, having grown up abroad, he also enjoyed an outsider's perspective. In Rangoon's information vacuum, I sometimes felt more isolated and ignorant of what was going on in Burma when I was there than when I was outside the country. The secrecy and inevitable self-censorship would warp my news judgement. While I can see in retrospect that interesting stories were dripping from the walls, in Rangoon's airless atmosphere I was often stuck for new ideas. 'Why don't you go and visit Thibaw's grandson?' Thant suggested. 'He lives up in Maymyo, I'm sure you can find him.'

Thibaw was the last king of Burma, ousted by the British when they annexed Upper Burma in 1885 and abolished Mandalay's Court of Ava. King Thibaw was a weak monarch, but thanks in part to the ruthless urges of his wife Queen Supayalat (who also happened to be his half sister), his brief reign was marked by brutal purges. Dozens of members of the extended royal family were imprisoned and later massacred – some, reputedly, were trampled under the feet of elephants. The new British rulers incorporated Burma into the Indian empire and banished Thibaw, Supayalat and their four daughters to the Indian coastal town of Ratnagiri, where they lived in comfortable yet diminished circumstances in a house on the Arabian Sea. In 1919, three years after Thibaw's death, Supayalat and her two unmarried younger daughters were allowed to return to Burma.

✿ ✿ ✿ ✿ ✿ ✿

Eighty-five-year-old Taw Paya, the sole surviving grandson of Thibaw and heir to the Konbaung throne, was living quietly in Maymyo. My guidebook had described the town's Home Counties feel and its colonial houses, most famously 'Candercraig', the 1920s turreted house which had served as the British officers' club and was now a government-run hotel. As it was *de rigueur* to avoid such state-run places, to avoid paying into the regime's coffers, I had chosen a smaller place in front of the lake, a fine red-brick house with mullioned windows, which would have once been home to a British civil servant and his family. I had been looking forward to my break from the city, but my romantic visions of a colonial nostalgia trip were soon doused when I entered the hotel's dingy formal dining room for breakfast. Any residual Raj-like charm had been extinguished by a boxed-in fireplace, brown nylon curtains and a garish lino floor. The square, teakwood tables were smothered with layers of yellow varnish. My breakfast too was disappointing, but perhaps not far from the colonial reality – a greying hardboiled egg, cold white toast with lurid yellow margarine, and sweet instant coffee.

❧ ✿ ✿ ✿ ✿ ✿ ❦

I cycled on past roadside nurseries selling colourful bedding plants. On a gentle rise, I was overtaken by a painted horse cart, driven by a man in a woolly jumper. At the next junction, empty of traffic, I took a right turn into Circular Road, into the heart of the colonial suburbs. Many of the mock-Tudor mansions were deserted, with signs of life concentrated around wooden shacks in the gardens, smoke rising from chimneys, laundry strung up, and bicycles, water drums and gas canisters parked outside. Territorial dogs charged down the overgrown lawns as I cycled past each generously appointed plot, snarling and growling around my ankles.

I knew Taw Paya lived on Forest Road near the Chinese temple, a bright yellow building with upturned eaves which came into view on my next turn. Loud rock music blared from speakers turned to face the street outside a newly built, open-fronted restaurant next door. Opposite was a large, Edwardian brick house, with a well-tended front garden bounded by a high wall. I rang the bell at the gate and the gardener who had been watering the flowerbeds dropped his hose and dashed over to let me in. I wheeled my bike up the driveway and parked it under the pansy-filled hanging baskets while the gardener called through the front door.

Two women came to meet me and, giggling, led me into the dark front room with its large fireplace and heavy wooden furniture. Through a curtained doorway, I could see through to the sunlight of the back garden and another woman crouching down and washing clothes in a wide plastic basin. We all sat, and I enquired about Taw Paya in my poor Burmese. They nodded and we waited. The washerwoman brought in some cold water in a glass jug with a crocheted doily on top. We waited for about half an hour more, until a man arrived, too young to be Taw Paya, and shook my hand. I attempted more questions. He left the room and after some minutes came back with a delicate, yellowed piece of paper, with looping Burmese writing. Could I be holding an ancient royal relic? I wasn't really sure what I was looking at, or who these people were, and I was starting to worry that I might be too late to meet Taw Paya. Were these his relatives, had he died? We engaged in another jumbled conversation. Finally, I understood. Taw Paya had moved house.

The young gardener hitched up his *longyi* and mounted his bike. I followed him up to Maymyo's main highway – a section of the famed Burma Road connecting Mandalay to China. We cycled north as heavy lorries and motorbikes overladen with Chinese rice cookers, kettles and electric fans whooshed past. Half a mile along, we turned off past a sports pitch into a more modern 1970s suburb, which, apart from the potholed, rubbly streets, was still very English in feel, the red-brick villas replaced by white dormer bungalows. We stopped outside a sliding metal gate and knocked. Finally I had found the king's grandson, in his own granny bungalow with PVC windows and net curtains.

~ ✿ ✿ ✿ ✿ ✿ ~

'Is that a gift?' he asked, tossing the box of biscuits on to the coffee table, very unimpressed. Like Maymyo's cool, fresh air, Taw Paya's forthright manner was a welcome novelty. His blue blood, combined with his advanced years, allowed him the privilege of speaking his mind, even when it came to talking about Burma's military rulers, a subject usually out of bounds for most Burmese people. Sitting in an armchair in a blue and black checked shirt and a sarong knotted high over his belly, he scoffed at the airs adopted by Burma's new elite. He spoke in quaint, clipped English, learned in mission schools in the 1930s. 'Those chaps, really, they are the ones who think they are royalty,' he said. 'They love big shows of wealth and power. But the people hate it. Ninety per cent of the people are poor. But they daren't say anything. This is a police state.' He looked a tiny bit worried. 'Where is this article going to be published? Will it be put on the Internet?'

When Taw Paya was growing up, the family lived on a modest but comfortable pension paid by the colonial administration. The king's daughters received 2,200 rupees per month, and his grandchildren 600 per month, enough to live simply and to pay for school fees. The British were concerned that the family could stir up nationalist fervour, and their movements were severely restricted. The young prince was educated in Rangoon and the southern port of Moulmein, and wasn't allowed to travel to the royal seat of Mandalay for inter-school football matches. The injustices still rankled. 'Mother died when I was twelve. The government did not allow me to visit our father. The British made sure we were all separated. National feeling was very strong in those days.'

At independence in 1948, the family lost their pension and for a few years, during the civil war that followed the end of the colonial era, they struggled. The gems and silverware that Thibaw and Supayalat had smuggled into exile in India had long been sold off or filched by British officers. The family had nothing but a few old black-and-white photographs to remind them of their royal heritage, now arranged neatly in frames on shelves behind where Taw Paya was sitting. In 1950, he and his surviving brother (communist insurgents had assassinated his elder brother shortly after independence) founded an import–export company, the Thibaw Commercial Syndicate, and in 1952 won a major tender to supply rice to India, a turning point that put the former royals within reach of middle-class prosperity. But it was not to last. In 1963, the firm, like all private companies in Burma, was nationalised by the new military government of General Ne Win.

The nationalisation of their business set the royal family on a track of downward mobility, their declining fortunes mirroring that of Burma itself, which slid down the league tables of economic prosperity. Taw Paya's four sons have led unexceptional lives – a boat builder, a security guard, a policeman and a driving instructor. His nephew, the great-grandson of King Thibaw, is a failed artist and down-and-out. 'Quite honestly, he lives in a mud hut,' Taw Paya told me, allowing himself a little chuckle. The heir to the throne himself had recently downsized to the bungalow, where his two daughters looked after him. He seemed happy with his lot. 'We have a TV in every room,' he said. 'And I'm very fond of the *Reader's Digest*.'

*~ ✿ ✿ ✿ ✿ ✿ ~*

Under its new name of Pyin Oo Lwin, the colonial haven of Maymyo grew as a military base under the junta's rule, as the home to the Defence Services Academy, Burma's equivalent of Sandhurst or West Point. The next morning, a Saturday, I sat in a coffee shop and watched young army cadets in white starched jackets wandering through town on their morning off, swinging plastic bags containing their purchases of toothpaste, biscuits and blankets. In the booth next to me, a pair of young soldiers sat in desultory conversation with two demure, beautiful, long-haired girls.

Each April, Burma's hottest month, the then junta leader Than Shwe would come to Maymyo for a holiday, and stay at Flagstaff, the residence built for the British commanding officers. 'When they come they bring a huge entourage,' said Taw Paya. 'The whole town is closed down.' Than Shwe's pretentions to royal status were well known. His palatial residence in Naypyidaw had pillars of jade and marble, and his family reputedly referred to each other using royal titles. Footage of his daughter's lavish 2006 wedding, leaked on to the Internet, showed the bride wearing a necklace of cherry-sized diamonds and her new husband pouring champagne over a cascade of glasses. At Flagstaff, the wives of the commanding officers would attend to Than Shwe's wife like ladies-in-waiting. The president's court would treat Maymyo like a playground, the prince said, commandeering taxis and restaurants with no suggestion of payment, and the wives of senior officers would get dolled up and walk around town, taking things from shops whenever they felt like it. 'They think they're entitled,' Taw Paya harrumphed.

Thibaw's living heir had no political aspirations. Would he like to be king? 'Don't be foolish. Politics is such a cheating game. I've never thought about it.' He did allow himself a little royal vanity, however. When we met, his life story had just been serialised in a popular Burmese women's magazine. Remembering this, he leapt up from his chair, rummaged through a pile of books and papers, and pulled out copies of the articles complete with black and white photos of his parents and grandparents. Scanning the Burmese text wistfully, he translated parts for my benefit. Taw Paya's identity was defined by events that occurred before his birth, and having it all laid out in print seemed to be a comfort. 'These articles were very popular actually,' he said, shyly. 'The sympathy for us is still quite strong.'

That evening, rather than face the dining room at the hotel, I went into town for dinner. The town's horse carts lined up in a rank by the Purcell clock tower, a gift from Queen Victoria. There were fruit and flower stalls, a well-lit shop selling baby clothes and plastic toys from China, a pharmacy and a photography studio. Several shops had knitted cardigans and sweaters hung up outside for sale – this was one of the few places in Burma where you would need them.

Maymyo has a large Gurkha population, descendants of colonial Indian Army soldiers who have lived in the town for generations. I followed a handmade sign to a small Nepalese restaurant on a back street behind the main shopping drag. The restaurant consisted of a few plastic tables on the ground floor of a wooden house with a bare dirt floor. Two women in saris were cooking in the back, and my waitress was a friendly girl in jeans and a jumper, who presented me with a feast of vegetable and chicken curries, pickles and chapattis on a stainless steel plate. I was the only customer, and the waitress stood right next to me and watched me eat. She had just completed a geography degree at Mandalay University. I told her I had studied geography too, in London. 'Really?' she said. 'I would like to go there. I would like to go there too and study geography again.' It would be expensive, I warned her, but there might be scholarships she could apply for. 'Oh, money is not a problem for us,' she said, sweeping her arm in a proprietorial arc across the dingy restaurant. 'This is all ours.'

# 6
# Born on 8.8.88

If Monk Owen hadn't left his village he would be spending each day cutting wood in the forest, looking forward to watching a Korean soap opera on the black-and-white TV, a night's sleep, then doing the same again the next day. His horizons would be bounded by the Irrawaddy River on one side, the forest on the other. He wouldn't have known that although its people were poor, Burma was rich in jade, teak and natural gas. He wouldn't have wanted to make a difference. Monk Owen is the perfect example of how education can change everything.

Owen's parents were woodcutters in the small village of Chaung Ma Gyi in Sagaing Division in upper Burma. When their second child, a boy, was delivered in their bamboo and thatch hut on the auspicious date of 8 August 1988, or 8.8.88, his mother was delighted. Astrology and numerology are highly significant in Burmese culture, and Owen's birthdate heralded good fortune for her firstborn son. Living in remote, rural Burma, with only the doctored news of the state television channel for information, Owen's mother did not know that on the very day she was giving birth, tens of thousands of demonstrators were on the streets of the Burmese capital Rangoon, demanding an end to one-party rule. Nor did she know that by the end of the day, a bloody crackdown had begun. News of the uprising wended its way up the four hundred and fifty miles of rutted highway, dirt track and silty river to reach the village in time for the baby boy's Buddhist naming ceremony, held, according to tradition, some three months after the birth. Sanda Kyaw Htin, 'Famous Brave Revolution', his proud mother named him, as a line of maroon-robed monks chanted from the holy texts.

If a sense of destiny surrounded Owen's entry into the world, his early years in the village were unremarkable. Like characters in a Grimm Brothers fairy tale, his mother and father, each armed with an axe, laboured in the forest all day. The children were left to roam the woods, climbing trees, sometimes fishing in the river. Each monsoon season, the rains would wash away the dirt road, leaving the village accessible only by the river. The family usually had enough to eat, but in lean times they would seek extra rice from the village's Buddhist monastery. Owen's infant years were carefree, but from an early age, he had a sense that something was missing. 'I knew I wasn't getting an education. I was very eager to learn. In the next village there were children who went to the government school, they wore green and white uniforms. I really wanted to go to school like them.' Although state-run schools in Burma are nominally free, the extra costs of uniforms, books and under-the-desk payments to teachers mean that the very poorest families cannot afford to enrol their children at school. The alternative for hard-up Buddhist parents is to send their offspring to monasteries as novice monks and nuns, where they are taught to read, write and memorise religious texts, subsisting on food collected in their black alms bowls. By the time he was eight years old, Owen had four younger siblings, and the family's economic situation was deteriorating fast. Owen's parents were left with little choice: they shaved their son's unruly black hair and packed him off to the whitewashed, gold-tipped monastery.

≈ ✿✿✿✿✿ ≈

The history of Buddhism in Burma is believed to date back more than two thousand years, to the Buddha's time. In the eleventh century, King Anawrahta introduced the Theravada tradition, practised by some 90 per cent of Burma's population today. It is a religion woven into the fabric of daily life. A column of serene, shaven-headed monks gliding down the roadside at daybreak is one of the country's enduring images. Burma has an estimated 400,000 monks, both those ordained for life, the *pongyi*, and boys whose families send them to the monastery as novices. Many Burmese men also take up temporary monastic residence later in life, and some return regularly for brief periods, as a kind of retreat. The Theravada school holds strictly to the teachings of Lord Buddha, as contained in a collection of his writings. Life as a monk is austere, with no possessions permitted except for their robes, velvet slippers and an alms bowl. A Buddhist monk should not eat after midday, should sleep on a hard surface, and eschew money and consumer goods. Buddhism esteems selflessness and good works, or 'making merit'. Although the clergy, the *sangha*, are in close contact with the Burmese people, on the streets, in the market, and even in private homes where they go to receive food offerings, they are the most revered members of society. A layperson must be careful not to step on a monk's shadow.

The fabled city of Mandalay, once the seat of Burmese kings, is the country's spiritual heart. Today it is a scrappy, low-rise sprawl, rising from the haze of the Irrawaddy plain. But it is also home to tree-shaded teak monasteries and tens of thousands of monks. In a tin-roofed teashop across the street from the walls of Phaung Daw Oo Monastery School, Monk Owen is sitting with his friends, a crimson-robed shoulder hunched over a glass of sugary tea. Behind him, a chef ladles the custardy mixture for rice pancakes on to an oily griddle, generating a perfect pile of air-filled mon' pyar thalet with a balletic economy of movement. The customers, including a group of uniformed police officers sitting cross-legged on the low plastic chairs, have an eye on a football match from the English Premiership – Fulham versus Liverpool on an LG flat-screen TV. Owen is twenty-three. He has a shaven head, of course, broad smooth cheeks, and the tilt of his chocolate-brown eyes suggest a perpetual smile. He has capable English; he keeps having to raise his voice to compete with the babble of the teashop, the excited football commentary, Burmese pop music and revving motorbikes on the street outside.

Owen grew to adolescence in the rural monastery. He was bored. He had read every spiritual text, every pamphlet and book he could find in the village. He still yearned to go to school. One day, a trader from Mandalay arrived, selling Chinese-made plastic goods – baskets, basins, pegs and twine. He came to the monastery to meditate. 'I asked him where I could go for an education for free,' said Owen, and the merchant promised he would make enquiries for him at the monastic school in the city. He was true to his word. The fairy tale had a happy ending. 'I was fifteen when I made it to Mandalay,' Owen told me. 'They tested my level of knowledge and I was put into the kindergarten with kids who were five years old. That's when my life began.'

Owen learned very quickly, and his first discovery was how little he knew. 'I didn't know anything about the world, about history, about my country,' he said. 'I didn't know anything beyond my forest and Buddha.' He eagerly sought out facts, inhaling information that he had missed out on in childhood. He practised his arithmetic, perfected his handwriting, studied maps and took an English dictionary to his sleeping mat after evening prayers. He asked a British woman visiting Phaung Daw Oo to give him an English name; she chose Owen. He sped through the academic years, and devoured the books in the monastic school's small library. He soon began to learn things about his country that made him angry. 'For example, I did not know that Burma is a rich country. It has many natural resources, but in our country the people are very poor, and the rulers are very rich.' He discovered that the military government's spending on weapons and defence dwarfed its budget for health and education. He found out that Burma used to be the world's greatest rice exporter but was now as poor as a sub-Saharan African nation. He lowered his voice conspiratorially. 'I read a lot. We have teakwood, jewels and natural gas. We have jade and rubber. Where does the money go?'

❧ ✿ ✿ ✿ ✿ ✿ ❧

Owen clutches my elbow and charts a dangerous course across a street busy with bicycles, speeding motorbikes (permitted in Mandalay), *saiq-kas* and overloaded commuter pickup trucks. We walk through the unmarked gate of the walled monastery. The harsh heat of the day is easing, and young novices, their robes tied up like bulky nappies, are playing football on the patch of open ground that sits beside a brand-new three-storey dormitory block, built with 'merit-making' donations. Their day's study and prayer over, groups of teenage monks lean out over the balconies, chatting and laughing. The school, which opened in the early 1990s, now has more than six thousand pupils, including two hundred and fifty novice nuns in their fine, pale pink robes. The children come from all over upper Burma, the sons and daughters of poor farmers from the northern states of Shan, Chin and Sagaing. They are the lucky ones; they have left behind illiterate parents and siblings for this golden opportunity of a free education. In the school office, open to the garden on two sides, a group of students is huddled around a large, old PC, and skinny cats stretch out in arcs on the warm marble floor. Bunches of bare electrical wires run across the top of the walls and a sign is taped next to a poster of the Lord Buddha.

*Here! The Children can pursue their studies cheerfully*
*Without charging entry fee or certificate fee*

*Without collecting monthly or yearly fee*
*Without receiving offertory for teachers*
*Any fee is not charged!*

The young monks rise at 4 a.m., wash their faces and clean the monastery for the first hour of the day. They go on their early morning alms round, collecting food in their bowls for breakfast and lunch. Breakfast is eaten at 8 a.m. The children study until midday, break for lunch (the remnants of their alms) and take lessons again until 4 p.m. The students meditate, pray and do their homework. It is a simple, disciplined day, but Owen feels greatly privileged. 'We are the fortunate ones,' he said. 'We are learning, as young people should. When I see children working in the teashop or picking up plastic bags and empty bottles I feel bad. It should not be like this. Burmese families cannot afford to send their children to school or look after them, so they go to work for a few kyat a day.'

From his study of Burma's recent history, Owen was aware that the education system, like every other sector of society, had been in decay. 'Fifty years ago, if you were an outstanding student, you would go to Rangoon University, one of the best in South-east Asia, and get a first-rate education. Now we have to send our best students to study in Singapore. We are left behind.' His unfolding education had also made him reflect on the parochialism of life back home. 'In my village the atmosphere is very small. They don't really know about the outside world. They only think about the living, the surviving,' he said. 'They go to the forest at five in the morning to cut wood, then come back at 11.30 and have lunch. At one o'clock they go back to the forest to cut wood, then they come back and cook dinner and watch a Korean soap opera on one TV for the whole village. At seven o'clock they go to bed; the whole family lies down together. That is their life.' Each year, the forest had retreated further and further from the village. The woodcutters were the architects of a local environmental disaster, but lacked the intellectual means to fathom it. Looking back from Mandalay, Owen could see things clearly. His anger towards the military government grew, for its neglect of its subjugated rural citizens. But, characteristically for such an energetic, ambitious young man, Owen decided to channel his anger into action.

In 2006, when he was just eighteen, and still ploughing through middle-school grades, Owen hatched a plan to establish a primary school in his home village, so no child would grow up uneducated as he did. He discussed his idea with an Italian visitor who came to Phaung Daw Oo. The tourist was sympathetic, and donated $300 to the cause, and with that Owen bought the bamboo and wood necessary to build a classroom and a latrine. Volunteers from the village helped to build the structure, attached to the village monastery. Owen persuaded four friends who had finished high school to be the teachers, promising them small salaries that he had no idea how he would pay. Mahasala Monastic Elementary School opened the following year, at the end of the hot season. Eighty-three children – who until that day had roamed the forest unsupervised – eagerly enrolled.

With just one classroom for all six elementary grades, when one class started, another had to stop. The roof leaked and the long-drop latrine collapsed in the rainy season. Owen was constantly trying to raise funds, to pay the teachers' salaries of thirty dollars a month, to build a new classroom and even some cement toilets. He told every visitor to the monastery about his school, showing them the small photo album he had compiled. He managed to attract interest, and funds, from the British embassy in Rangoon as well as some hefty sums from exiled Burmese and private donors in Canada, Germany and Spain. Owen, who could have been leading the carefree life of any young student, now had the very adult responsibilities of managing money, paying employees, setting the curriculum and planning the future of an ever-expanding school. Why did he do it? 'I knew that in my village there was no future for kids like me. We are Buddhist so we have to help each other,' he said simply. 'Building the school was not my choice.'

☙ ✿ ✿ ✿ ✿ ✿ ❧

Grounded in a philosophy of enlightenment, nonviolence and rebirth, Buddhism traditionally embraces peace, clarity and wisdom — attributes of the Buddha who lived some 2,500 years ago. However, throughout Burma's history, this has not precluded a strong role in politics for the *sangha*. Successive governments have sought validation from the Buddhist clergy, making generous donations for the construction of temples and pagodas. But the monks are known better for their subversive role. Sheathed in their iconic robes, they have been at the forefront of Burma's struggle for democracy and, before that, independence.

During the uprisings of recent decades, monks were centre stage, both in 1988 when they supported strikes and demonstrations and in 2007, when they led peaceful protests across the country. Burma's generals, recognising the monks' power, tried to appease them by giving lavishly to individual clergy, donating to monasteries and spending millions of dollars restoring Buddhist temples. They cultivated a faction of loyal monks to whom they could offer alms, a practice necessary to safeguard their authority. But many in the *sangha* resented the association. In 1999, the generals regilded the spire of the Shwedagon pagoda with more than fifty tons of gold and thousands of diamonds. An earthquake shook Rangoon during the reconstruction, which senior monks interpreted as a sign of divine displeasure with the regime.

In the Saffron Uprising of 2007, Owen joined the monks marching in Mandalay to call for democracy. 'The demonstrations of '88 started on the day I arrived on the planet. By the time of the next demonstration I was already fully grown. But nothing had changed.' Owen's teacher had a computer. They typed up posters to organise the city's monks, telling them when and where to meet to start the demonstrations. 'We told our fellow monks it was their duty to join us.' Every morning at about nine, the monks would start their march, the numbers swelling each day from thousands to tens of thousands. The army blocked the roads with barbed wire; Mandalay's mayor came to talk to beg the young clergy not to demonstrate, he said he had orders to shoot if necessary. But in cities across Burma, the monks continued to march, becoming recognised around the world as a symbol of peaceful resistance. Some appeared on the streets with their alms bowls turned upside down, signalling that they would refuse the military's merit-making offerings, an act tantamount to ex-communication. The uprising ended when troops shot dead protestors, disrobed and imprisoned monks, and shut down dozens of monasteries.

In 2007, the reputation of the Burmese monkhood, a cherished and peace-loving institution, was at its height, just as the standing of the military government was at an all-time low. But over the coming years, that was to change; the accepted picture of good versus evil would start to blur as elements of the Buddhist clergy in Burma became associated with extremist, anti-Muslim ideology.

✿ ✿ ✿ ✿ ✿ ✿

We climb up to the third floor of the teaching block, to an unused classroom with desks daubed with Tippex graffiti pushed into one corner and wooden chairs piled up on top of them. We are escaping the inquisitive attention of the young novices who crowd around us as I try to learn more about Owen's life, repeating every question I ask, enjoying the feel of English words in their mouths. 'So, how many students do you have now?' I ask him. 'So, how many students do you have now?' parrot the young monks, their tone more reverent than cheeky. 'And what will you do when you finish school?' The boys chant their echo. Owen shoos them off with a sharp admonishment and they scamper away, making no sound in their bare feet. We go into the building and up the flights of concrete steps. A crackly Justin Bieber song floats up the stairwell. Through a cracked window we look out over the rooftops and palm fronds of Mandalay's skyline in the coppery evening light, the ridge of the Shan hills on the eastern horizon.

Owen has just matriculated from high school, passing his Standard 10 examinations with strong grades. He is eager to improve himself in a bigger world. He has applied to university, to major in English. He has recently returned from an exploration of north-eastern Burma, towards the Chinese border, which he made on a borrowed motorbike. There he visited the ruby mines of the Mogok valley, and spoke to farmers from the Shan and Lisu ethnic groups whose land had been confiscated to make way for mining. Like every new piece of knowledge about the workings of the Burmese economy, it has fuelled his feelings of injustice. I ask him whether he will remain as a monk. He hasn't decided yet. 'I want to become president, or a great monk to help my country. One of those. I'm not sure. I really want to be the president and if I want to be the president then I can't be a monk.' If you become president what will your policies be; what do you want to achieve? Owen's campaign message is simple. 'I want to open a lot of schools in this country,' he says. 'That's what I will do when I am president. Each week I will open a school, and I won't stop until everyone has an education for free.'

# 7
# A Bamboo City

A quick pencil sketch of Burma's ethnic topography situates the dominant Burman group on the broad central plain and the fertile delta, with the minority Shan, Mon, Karen, Karenni, Chin, Kachin and Arakanese groups scattered in the hills to the east, north and west. Burma boasts a startling human diversity, home to an officially estimated 135 ethnic groups. Migration to the cities, to more fertile lands and mining regions has complicated this back-of-an-envelope depiction, but in general, the same ethnic delineations that British colonialists found in the nineteenth century still exist today.

Historically, many of these mountain communities enjoyed a measure of self-rule, or were even untouched by Burman authority completely. Before the British imperialists agreed to grant Burma independence, they insisted that the political status of non-Burman groups of the borderlands be resolved. In February 1947, General Aung San, the architect of Burma's independence, brought together ethnic leaders in the small town of Panglong in the breezy Shan hills, with the aim of devising a political structure acceptable to both Burmans and minority nationalities. Although the Karen leaders boycotted the conference, the agreement that the Chin, Kachin and Shan signed with Aung San guaranteed ethnic minorities equal rights and a degree of autonomy within a federal system. But the general was assassinated later that year, and the Panglong Accord was never implemented. In fact, following independence in 1948, Burma's new rulers sought to rein in more political and economic power to the centre, efforts which the people of the periphery resisted with an explosion of armed struggles – collectively waging what has become the world's longest-running civil war.

Beginning in the 1960s, the military government implemented a policy known as the Four Cuts, with the aim of eliminating all forms of support to insurgent forces by cutting their access to food, intelligence, money and recruits. Campaigns by the Burmese army, the Tatmadaw, particularly in the Karen and Kachin hills, killed tens of thousands of people and forced many more to flee their land. By the mid-1990s, the regime had negotiated ceasefire deals with seventeen resistance groups across Burma, but the guerrilla soldiers of the Karen National Union (KNU) refused any compromise, and continued to fight. The relationship between the Karen, of Mongolian descent, and the ethnic Burmans, distantly related to the Tibetans and Chinese, has an acrimonious history. The Karens enjoyed preferential treatment under colonial rule and sided with the British during the Second World War, while the Burmans welcomed invading Japanese forces as their liberators. Burman and Karen villagers massacred each other in tit-for-tat attacks. By the end of the war, Burman allegiance had switched to the Allies, but both British colonial policies and the bloodletting of the war left a legacy of mistrust between Burmans and the Karen, who continued to fight for their own independent homeland. In 1949, a KNU uprising against the Burman-led government saw Karen troops seize control of several cities in central Burma and even the northern suburbs of Rangoon, before being driven back to their eastern mountain strongholds from where they continued their decades-long struggle.

☙ ✿ ✿ ✿ ✿ ✿ ❧

Mu Mu, a Karen from the eastern hills, was not happy down in the Burmese lowlands. While my experience of Rangoon's teashops and markets was of polite attention and kindnesses, Mu Mu encountered rudeness and slights. Her high cheekbones, her fine, straight nose, her accent marked her out as a hill person in the city. She told me how she asked a shopkeeper for directions and was ignored, how a hairdresser was rude to her, cab drivers refused to pick her up. In Bangkok she had friends, a community and her faithful mobile phone. Rangoon was technically home, but an alien place. Although she could eat her favourite childhood breakfast of rice and steamed beans, she saw no charm, as we did, in the city's crumbling buildings, its Second World War buses, its pedicabs and wooden monasteries. After Bangkok, Rangoon was backward. A SIM card for a mobile phone, available for three dollars in every 7-Eleven in Thailand, still cost thousands of dollars in Burma. Instead of the sky train and smooth, air-conditioned taxis, there were heaving, overloaded pickup trucks. Mu Mu was nervous, too; we were never to mention her life in Bangkok or her friends in the refugee camps. She kept her distance from the other nannies who looked after our children's friends, and rarely shared stories about her past. She spent her weekends in the Internet cafés of Yankin shopping mall, talking by Skype to her friends in Thailand. She was lonely.

Her decision to leave came after such a call from her childhood friend Wan in the Mae La refugee camp, just inside Thailand near the border town of Mae Sot. Wan, like thousands of other young people in the camp, was hoping to make it to a 'third country' – America, Canada, Australia or Norway – through the United Nations resettlement programme that had already found Mu Mu's former boyfriend Saw Myo a new home in Vancouver. Camp dwellers were given little solid information, but rumours spread quickly and there were regular bouts of excitement and expectation when signs of heightened activity by UN staff were spotted. The hopeful migrants decided that this was at last the moment when they would set out to a new land, to start a new life. The telephone trees would swing into action to disseminate the news; mobile phones would buzz in homes across Bangkok to alert those who had signed up in the camps but slipped away to earn money in the city, leaving trusted friends and relatives behind to inform them of any signs that bureaucratic wheels were turning. Mu Mu got the same message. 'Come now, something is really happening this time!' Wan told her. It was another big decision for Mu Mu, but an opportunity she could not pass up. She packed her two small suitcases and thought about America. A new life and a new beginning.

❧ ✿ ✿ ✿ ✿ ✿ ❧

Mu Mu thought she knew what to expect – she had already spent three weeks in a camp when she had chased after Saw Myo. But in her heartbroken state she had taken little of it in, now she saw things with fresh eyes. Mae La was home to 45,000 people, the population of a small city, but a ban on any permanent construction meant the sprawling settlement was built entirely from wood, bamboo and thatch. Single-roomed shanties, woven from flimsy bamboo strips and perched on stilts to protect them from the muddy torrents of the wet season, were set along unpaved, rutted trails that ran up and down hillsides now denuded of trees. Women cooked on charcoal burners, squatting by them and fanning away smoke that drifted up to cling to damp laundry strung up between houses. Circles of boys were playing *chin lone*, keeping the wicker balls aloft with their heads, knees and feet, mud spattered up their bare shins. On one corner, under a shelter made of blue plastic sheeting, a group of men gathered around a television screen, watching Italian league football. Two women sat on their stoop, one unhurriedly rummaging through the other's hair in search of ticks. The camp smelt of ash and sewage. Mu Mu looked about her, struck by the engulfing sense of inertia. Everyone here was marking time.

The once thickly-forested hillsides of Mae La in Thailand's Tak province were first settled in the mid-1980s by refugees escaping the state-sanctioned abuses against the hill peoples for which Burma became infamous – forced labour, gang rape, land grabs and village raids. The first exodus was triggered by an incursion by the Tatmadaw into territory traditionally held by Karen fighters, followed by revenge attacks on civilians branded as rebel sympathisers. Villages were looted and burnt, women raped, and young men forced to work as unpaid porters for the army. The next wave came in 1988, when the student-led uprising in Rangoon was violently crushed, and thousands fled across the border to escape reprisals and plot their next moves against the military government. Over the following two decades, spikes in migration across the border corresponded to surges in fighting and attacks on civilians. From 2005, the escapees were joined by another breed of refugee, those like Mu Mu and her friends, not running directly from danger but fleeing Burma's economic ruins. The camp was not their new home, but a staging post, they hoped, to a new life overseas.

'When I got there I found my name was not on the list,' Mu Mu told me later. 'So I had to buy a place.' Mu Mu had money saved, all she needed to do was pay off someone whose name was on the United Nations list, and assume their identity. In a camp where no one had a passport, few had ID cards, and many Burmese names were drawn from a limited repertoire (each person would likely share their name with dozens of others), this was a straightforward operation. The camp dwellers could be broadly divided into two categories: those keen to get out, and those content to stay. The children and grandchildren of the first generation of escapees had known no other life. The razor wire surrounding the camp marked the perimeter of their world – many had never stepped outside. In the camp, the United Nations staff ensured they were given sufficient rations of rice, oil and beans. Most of Mae La's inhabitants were Karen, and many of them Christian – Baptists and Seventh Day Adventists whose forebears had been converted by nineteenth-century missionaries. Well-funded American ministries and other Western charities had a strong presence in the camps, ensuring there were good schools, nurseries and medical clinics. With their essential needs met, there were plenty of volunteers who were delighted to receive a few thousand Thai baht in return for relinquishing the opportunity to start a new life in Utah or Vancouver – places they had never heard of and had no desire to see.

Mu Mu secured her place on the list, and turned her attention to finding somewhere to live. This was the first time in her adult life that she was doing something just for herself, for her own future. She stopped sending money home; her efforts to sort out the financial problems of her feckless parents had yielded little success. 'I told them I couldn't help them any more. I told them to sell the house. It was all they had left,' Mu Mu said. 'I had to talk to them like I was the parent and they were the children. In Burma we don't talk to our parents like this.' As profligate as her parents had been, she still found it hard to wash her hands of them. Her youngest sister Hla Hla had followed in her footsteps and had found a position as a domestic worker in Bangkok – she would become the family breadwinner for now. Mu Mu slept on the floor of her friend Wan's house for a few weeks, and then spent her savings on her own bamboo hut – her very first home of her own. She found beauty in her new life in this strange cocoon on a Thai hillside, with its fresh, clear days and candlelit nights. 'It was cool at night, so beautiful,' she recalled. 'It was cheap there, we had no worries. We didn't need new clothes or anything like that. We got just enough food. It was a simple life.'

While it was possible to subsist with no cash at all in the camp, Mu Mu missed having an income. The refugees were not permitted to step beyond the camp's perimeter fence to find work, and doing so would mean running the gauntlet of the Thai security guards who would demand bribes from the men and sexual favours from the women. Any formal business activity inside the camps was forbidden by the authorities, but of course the more industrious and entrepreneurial bent the rules and set up their own small enterprises: beauty salons, electrical repair shops, carpentry and food stalls. Mu Mu got a job working in a makeshift crisp factory, run from one of the shacks, where potatoes were peeled, chopped, fried, salted and bagged. It was piece work: Mu Mu was paid half a Thai baht for each bag she filled, and aimed for fifty bags each day, giving her twenty-five baht, or around seventy cents – just enough for her to buy small luxuries such as shampoo, Internet time, or a pirated DVD to watch on her friend's laptop. Mu Mu's task was to sit and fill up the clear plastic bags with their greasy contents. It was the first sedentary job she had ever had. 'I was sitting all day long, I started to get fat. I was eating the crisps and not moving at all.' Mu Mu was waiting, biding her time. She knew this wouldn't be for ever, and she kept her sights on her goal, day-dreaming about life in America, the little house she would live in, the car she would buy, all the while filling her bags of crisps, one after another.

Mu Mu recalls the optimism of that time, the sudden bursts of excitement and chatter in the camp when it seemed that the next group of people was about to be selected for resettlement. 'It's coming soon, it's going to be soon!' her friends would tell Mu Mu. More countries had offered new homes to the Karen refugees – New Zealand, the Netherlands, the Czech Republic and Japan. Her best friend Wan had made the cut. Wan had recently married her childhood sweetheart in a ceremony complete with a white satin dress, a professional wedding video and food and drink for scores of relatives – paid for by the bride from her job looking after two Dutch children in Bangkok. Now she and her new husband were heading for northern California after taking part in cultural orientation classes which taught them how to use an electric stove, what to pack in a suitcase, coping with cold and the best way to eat pizza. Mu Mu went to the camp gate to watch her friend leave. Wan's face was pressed up against the window of the bus, tears in her eyes. She raised her hand in a half-executed wave. Mu Mu stood still, her plastic flip-flops slowly sinking in the mud, for a long time after the bus had pulled away and the crowd around it had dispersed. Mu Mu was happy for Wan, but she couldn't help wondering when her time would come.

# 8
# Bones Will Crow

Afterwards he found out it was a week. He was hooded and handcuffed the whole time, beaten and questioned, woken from sleep, punched, kicked, tormented. Later in his prison life his knowledge of time would become a point of pride, but in that first week, drowning in its constant darkness, he lost track of it.

Win Tin was arrested on the morning of Tuesday 4 July 1989, and arrived at Rangoon's Insein prison at around 3 p.m. 'They went through my details, and when they had written everything in the book, I was taken to my cell. It was Block 2, cell number 54.' The single-storey cellblocks at the sprawling, British-built prison radiated from a central tower. Most of them faced to the outside, across a triangle of scrubby ground to the next block. But in Block 2, the brick cells faced inwards to a dark corridor and a cell opposite. This block was usually reserved for condemned prisoners. 'In death row, the rooms were facing each other. They had metal gates, not solid doors. This was so if someone tried to commit suicide, someone else would see it. But no one was around me, the cell opposite was empty, the cells around me were empty.'

Darkness fell quickly just after six. An hour later, they came to his cell, prison officials and intelligence officers. A group of them, he couldn't remember how many. The thick, rough, hessian hood went on. His hands were cuffed behind his back. He was marched off to another room – a small windowless room, he believed, from the heat, the air, the acoustics. And then it began.

'They came in one after another and asked questions and questions. If I didn't answer, if I didn't say what they wanted, I was knocked and kicked and beaten. This was my first experience of such behaviour. I was a well-known journalist, not a brute or a thug.

'I was resigned. I had no feeling at all. Someone would beat me and leave. Then a new man would come in. I would say I have just been beaten, and the officer would say "No you haven't. That didn't happen. That didn't happen to you." I didn't know who was doing it. I had no witness.'

Win Tin, then a reasonably fit fifty-nine-year-old, was given no food at all, just sips of water. After what was probably several days, he was given some rice to eat, but by then he was beyond eating. His stomach growled, but his head felt no hunger. Sometimes they took him to a room and told him to sit and stay silent. Then they would bring in other dissidents – his friends and colleagues from the National League for Democracy – and interrogate them while he listened. The others were hooded too; they didn't know he was there. 'They gave accounts of meetings we had and things I was supposed to have said,' Win Tin told me. 'It was not their fault, they were forced to do it.' Through nineteen years of imprisonment, through all the blows and kicks, Win Tin refused to betray his colleagues. But in his instinctively generous way, he was completely sympathetic to those who succumbed.

The seventh day was the day of his court hearing. When Win Tin arrived at the courthouse he was broken. All he could do was lie down on the floor. His upper teeth had been kicked in, his speech laboured and mumbled. Win Tin's niece was allowed to see him, she had brought him clean clothes. When she helped him to change, she saw the black and purple welts across his body. She demanded that he tell the court he had been tortured. No, he said, exhausted but resolute. If people know this, if the young men and women who want to join our democracy movement know this, they may be afraid. I cannot stop our movement. But what about truth, what about justice? 'Bones will crow,' he told his niece. He was convinced that one day, even if he died, the truth would be told.

❦ ✿ ✿ ✿ ✿ ✿ ❧

I first met Win Tin in the Sky Bistro on the top floor of Rangoon's Sakura Tower. It was an upmarket place with air conditioning, piped music and panoramic views of the city – the golden Shwedagon, the patched up roofs of colonial apartment blocks, the muddy Rangoon River and green fields of Dala beyond. It was a year since his release, but the country was still locked under military rule. A noisy French family, tourists taking refuge from the heat, were at the next table, reviewing the day's photographs on a professional-looking Canon. They didn't recognise Win Tin, but the dinner-jacketed waiters murmured to each other and looked admiringly at the white-haired gentleman ripping open little paper sachets and stirring sugars into his coffee. I was sitting at right angles to him at the square table, hunched up and nervous; being with this well-known opposition leader in a public place was a risk. A few minutes into our conversation, one of the waiters came to the table and pushed a folded piece of paper towards me across the starched tablecloth. I opened it and read the neat handwriting. 'Do not look round,' it began. 'I am seated behind you. I am a Japanese journalist and I would like to meet Mr Win Tin at a secure location. Please tell him to call me at my hotel, at this number, but only on a secure line.' I was already feeling protective of the charming Win Tin and was irritated by the instructional tone of the message. I passed it across the table. Win Tin read it and laughed. 'Everyone is so full of fear!' he said. By then, he had nothing left to be frightened of.

Win Tin was a glamorous figure with thick hair, a handsome square face, and glasses with chunky, black frames which were back in fashion, whether he was aware of it or not. Many of Burma's younger political prisoners liked to say they were the age they would have been if they subtracted the lost years they spent in prison. This applied nicely to the octogenarian Win Tin, who, despite his fragile health, had an impish movement and the manner of a much younger man. He was carelessly stylish with his open-necked shirt, tank top and *longyi*, all in blue, the regulation prison colour that he had insisted on wearing since his release from jail as a form of protest against the continued incarceration of many other prisoners of conscience. He carried a woven Shan sling bag that contained his phone, glasses case and a small bundle of kyat. Silver bangles jangled on his lean forearms.

He was happy to talk about his life. His genteel English betrayed his colonial schooling; his memory sometimes failed him for a moment and he strained to recall a name or word, but usually found it. After that first encounter at Sakura Tower, we met for three, long interviews during the peak of the hot season in April 2011, in the tense, unforgiving weeks before the monsoon brings relief. Each time, we sat at one end of a heavy teak table in the conference room of the NLD office in Rangoon. Orange nylon curtains were drawn against the afternoon sun. There were frequent interruptions – the communications officer with the first draft of a new party treatise, a former general returning a borrowed book on Buddhist meditation, the tea lady fussing around. Filing cabinets were crammed around the edge of the room, the overspill of folders piled messily on top. The pale green paint was peeling from the moist walls. There were eighteen straight-backed wooden chairs with faded embroidered cushions and one ancient air conditioner, which didn't work. Win Tin seemed oblivious to the suffocating heat, but as my recordings of the interviews attest, I didn't cope well at all, apologetically gulping down water and even requesting breaks so I could stand at the open window in search of fresh air. As my interviewee recounted stories of torture and fortitude, the irony of my feebleness in the face of a little heat was not lost on me. Thankfully, the former prisoner didn't seem to register my discomfort, and his words spilled out, punctuated only by his intermittent, hacking cough.

❧ ✿ ✿ ✿ ✿ ✿ ❧

Win Tin was born in the small market town of Gyo Pin Gauk on 12 March 1930, just a few months before the Buddhist monk Saya San launched the first revolt against British rule. Burma has rarely been at peace since. Win Tin lived through Second World War bombings and the Japanese occupation, communist insurrections and armed mutinies, two military coups, popular uprisings and the ethnic insurgencies in Burma's borderlands. At the age of thirteen, at the height of the war in the Far East, he was sent to a local monastery to be ordained as a novice monk. It was a happy time. Win Tin enjoyed the simplicity, the orderliness, and submitting to the collective. It was possibly this experience that inspired him to decide at an early age to devote his life to society, to the exclusion of all else. 'I am a single person. I have no family life. Most of my life I have lived for my work, as a politician and a journalist. That has consumed my life. Since the age of about nineteen I have lived as a public man. By that I don't mean as a well-known person; I mean that my life belongs to society, and society is my life.'

He was an instinctive journalist. If there was information, Win Tin wanted to share it. (Many of his imprisoned colleagues who missed out on the digital revolution during years of incarceration emerged wary of new technology. But Win Tin had embraced it – his smart phone was his new, constant companion.) When Burma's civil war broke out in 1948, Win Tin had already entered the University of Rangoon. It was not safe to go back to his hometown, some one hundred and twenty miles north of the city. He stayed in the capital and in 1950 found work – by day at the Burma Translation Society, while also putting in shifts as the night editor for Agence France Press. A few years later, he won a scholarship to go to the Netherlands as a journalism apprentice. He found it lonely, but focused on learning as much as he could in this strange, new environment. Mimicking the reporting techniques of George Orwell, he moved lodgings frequently, living in a working-class suburb, then a wealthy neighbourhood 'just to know how people are'. One carefree summer, he hitchhiked his way around Europe, from England to Greece.

At that time, Win Tin was the only Burmese in the Netherlands. He thought about other expatriates in Europe and the United States – mostly students and junior doctors – who might be longing for news from home. He had plenty of sources in Burma who were writing to him with news, none of it good. Burma was unstable. The economy was in pieces. The countryside had been carved up into territories controlled by rival rebel groups or government loyalists. Chinese nationalist soldiers roamed the Shan hills. Amid the chaos, rice exports had slumped, and the timber mills, oil wells and jade mines of British rule barely functioned. Win Tin tracked down a company in Germany that produced typewriters with the Burmese script. He hitched a lift across the border and returned with one, typed up his first four-page newsletter and copied it with a Cyclostyle machine. He posted the newsletter to all the addresses he had, and constantly sought out more readers, topping up his mailing list. He imagined the young men (and handful of women) feeling lonely in their lodgings in Sheffield or Berkeley. 'Even if people lived in the same house or the same room I would send them their own copy by name,' he said. 'When you are abroad, it is nice to get something addressed especially to you.'

By the time he returned to Burma in 1957, Win Tin had already been marked out as a dissident. He set up several newspapers, some of which were closed down or suspended. In 1968, at the time of the Prague Spring, the information ministry, nervous about his influence, banished him to Mandalay, hoping a provincial posting would quieten him. But Mandalay was a city of writers, poets and students, with a radical buzz, which Win Tin instantly embraced. He would sit in a pavement teashop, on a wooden stool under the shade of a tamarind tree, discussing political ideas. He found himself freer, and, as editor-in-chief of the widely read *Hanthawaddy Daily*, his influence grew. At nine o'clock each night an editor from the state censor – the Press Scrutiny Board – would call to go through the sentences or articles to be deleted from the following day's paper. 'He called from Rangoon, and of course in those days the line was not too good,' said Win Tin. 'Sometimes I would just not pick up the phone. Sometimes I would say, "Sorry, I can't hear you very well," and publish the stuff anyway.'

Win's Tin's political connections afforded him some latitude. The country's leader, Ne Win, liked him. Having seized power in the 1962 coup, the army general had brought an end to Burma's post-independence chaos, but was now gaining a new reputation as an autocrat and an economic bungler. Ne Win's 'Burmese Way to Socialism', which combined elements of extreme nationalism, Marxism and Buddhism, was helping to ensure that the country was making none of the economic progress of its neighbours. The free press was crushed, and most high-profile journalists were locked up. Despite his reputation as a bluff military strongman, however, Ne Win had an intellectual side and sought out the company of the original, freethinking Win Tin. Each time he came to Mandalay, usually en route to his summer residence in the hill station of Maymyo, the general would invite the journalist for dinner. Win Tin cared little for the dictator, but used the improbable relationship to his advantage. 'It was a great safeguard for me,' Win Tin said. 'Because the authorities knew of my contact with Ne Win, they didn't dare be too harsh.'

By the late 1980s, Win Tin was one of Burma's most prominent journalists and head of the Journalists' Union. Like so many of the country's brightest and best, he was swept up in the unrest of 1988, when students marched down the streets shouting democracy slogans, workers from lawyers to dock labourers went on strike, and revolutionary politics were openly discussed in hurriedly printed pamphlets and impromptu meetings in tea shops. The year before, Burma had been designated by the United Nations as one of the world's least developed nations. That same year, without warning, the government had taken the twenty-five, thirty-five and seventy-five kyat notes out of circulation. There was no exchange of old bills for new; families lost their cash savings overnight. As became the pattern in Burma, it took an economic shock in an already desperately poor country to push people on to the streets. The demonstrations began on Rangoon's university campuses. On 16 March 1988, students marched between the city's two major universities,

Rangoon University and the Rangoon Institute of Technology. They were cornered by soldiers and police near Inya Lake. Some fled, some were shot and beaten to death, some driven into the lake to drown. Another forty-one students suffocated to death in a police van outside Insein Prison, and hundreds more were arrested. On 23 July, General Ne Win resigned, only to be replaced by General Sein Lwin, the head of the riot police. The pro-democracy protests intensified.

Forty-three-year-old Aung San Suu Kyi, the daughter of Burma's independence hero, was back in Burma from her home in Oxford to nurse her mother, who had suffered a stroke. She spent her days at her mother's bedside in Rangoon General Hospital, but was becoming increasingly involved in the protest movement. She arranged a meeting with the Journalists' Union to discuss the unfolding events. 'She was a famous man's daughter, but she had no experience at all, she was just a housewife,' Win Tin recalled. By August, when students and workers united in a general strike that paralysed the government, she was meeting with the union every day. It took a while for Win Tin to recognise Suu Kyi's leadership qualities, and it wasn't until a mass rally on 26 August, when the revolutionary's daughter made her first public speech, that he was fully convinced. 'We had already seen she had a sharp mind, and that she was a lively person with a jolly sense of humour, and very intelligent too. But I didn't know whether she was good enough to be a political leader until she made the speech at Shwedagon. Her talk was very clear, straightforward. She was concise and very precise. Her Burmese was perfect, and she never dropped in English words, which is a bad habit of many people here. We were all completely taken with her.'

From then on, Win Tin and Suu Kyi worked closely together. The activists held talks with the government, but hopes for a smooth political transition were ruptured by the 18 September coup against the ruling Burma Socialist Programme Party. A new military order, the self-styled State Law and Order Restoration Council (SLORC), took over, and soldiers were quickly deployed across the country, breaking up strike centres and blockades. Nine days later, in response to the renewed crackdown, the National League for Democracy was formed, becoming the democracy struggle's most recognised political movement. Win Tin was one of its founders, along with Suu Kyi and retired General Tin Oo. One of Win Tin's jobs as party secretary was to transcribe Suu Kyi's speeches for publication. 'It was never necessary to edit the speeches or change the syntax, it was always perfect,' he recalled. 'One of the things I admire about her is her ability to talk to the people and cut through to what is important.' The momentum was strong, and hundreds of thousands joined the party in months. Excited by his new political role, Win Tin began to read the works of Henry Thoreau, who had conceived the philosophy of civil disobedience – an argument advocating individual resistance to government to draw attention to unjust rule. He was struck by the ideas, and believed Thoreau's political thinking could be a force for change in Burma. 'No government can wage a war if no one believes in it,' he said. In June 1989, Win Tin started a movement of civil disobedience, travelling the country to urge people to join the cause. It took only a month for him to be arrested.

❧ ✿ ✿ ✿ ✿ ❧

Win Tin was convicted of charges including spreading anti-government propaganda and sentenced to three years in prison. Internationally, it was a time of both crackdown and emerging freedom. Just weeks before, Chinese troops had massacred demonstrators in Tiananmen Square. But in Poland, voters had elected a new, Solidarity-led government, and in South Africa, President P.W. Botha met the imprisoned Nelson Mandela for the first time. With fresh charges piled upon him while in prison, Win Tin, one of thousands of pro-democracy activists imprisoned by the Burmese junta, would not be freed for nineteen and a half years. Nearly all of his prison life was spent in solitary confinement. The pain of isolation was intense, and he suffered physical agony as well. For the first eight years of his incarceration he had no teeth. 'In one beating in the first week I lost all the front teeth in my upper jaw. My other teeth were weak and broken. After four or five months a dentist came and removed all of my teeth, except for a few in the lower jaw. I asked for dentures – at my own expense, of course – but for years they refused.'

The staple prison food was low grade, chewy brown rice. 'Because the rice was so hard, I couldn't eat very well. I would try to soften it with my gums. But my eating ability diminished. My stomach contracted. I suffered. I can only eat three or four spoonfuls of rice, even now.'

Win Tin was always kept apart from others. He would be separated from another occupied cell by three or four empty chambers, to make talking difficult. If he was taken out to exercise in the yard, he was taken alone. His meagre meals were passed to him through the bars of the cell. During the few spells he spent in Insein's prison hospital, he was kept apart from the other patients. Psychologically, he was never broken, but it took him a while to acclimatise to his new environment. In 1992, an NLD member, Aung Kyaw Oo, who was elected to parliament in the 1990 general election (the junta had ignored the result), was installed in a cell a few doors down from Win Tin in Block 3, to where the former journalist had been moved. They made some contact, calling out to each other after lockdown. They tried to befriend the guards, giving away the milk powder and coffee delivered to them by friends and family in fortnightly packages.

The guards began to allow Win Tin, Aung Kyaw Oo and the other prisoners a little contact with each other. Sometimes they could share a few words as they took their toilet pails to empty in the latrine in the morning, and after lockdown in the evening they would chat through the bars of their cells. Win Tin, a community organiser his whole life, tried to formalise the arrangement – setting up committees, electing representatives, trying to make things better; it was in his blood. Win Tin always felt responsibility for others. 'We decided to create a movement in the prison in two tiers. The first was the social tier.' From 6.30 to 8.30 in the evening, the inmates of Block 3 – all of them political prisoners – would sing, tell stories and share experiences, all through the bars of their cells. They got to know each other. They would celebrate birthdays, pooling their supplies of salt, sugar, tea and coffee powder from the visitors' care packages to give as a gift.

Next came the 'political tier'. After two months, the prisoners made plans to set up a Joint Action Committee. Win Tin was excited when he told me: it was clear that this had been the point when the adrenalin of politics had begun to flow again. The prisoners came from many political backgrounds: there was Ko Jimmy, a famous student leader of the '88 uprising, communists, ethnic politicians from Karen and Shan parties, members of the Democratic New Society party, and the NLD. But politics had to adapt to prison conditions. 'We decided against taking adversarial positions, but to operate by consensus, this was the only way it could work in prison. Political life was a bit different there, not everything depended on doctrine and ideology. We had to make allowances. Sometimes people would feel depressed, sometimes they were in a bad mood. Sometimes they just weren't strong enough to cooperate.'

The committee started producing pamphlets of three or four pages, discussing political ideas and current affairs. They would ask visitors for news of the political situation outside and write it down. Sometimes they would smuggle in newspapers, or parts of newspapers, hidden in bowls of rice brought by relatives. 'The paper was dirty and oily, but we would clean it and read it, then we could use the paper again,' Win Tin said. 'We were always short of paper. Our activities helped to boost our morale: focusing on this kind of thing stopped us from becoming distorted and depressed.' Over the years visitors smuggled in letters, books and magazines. In the other direction, the prisoners sent out letters to loved ones, reports on prison life, and even submitted a dispatch to the United Nations, detailing abuses at Insein. The guards were bribed with milk powder and cheroots to turn a blind eye. Emboldened by their success, the prisoners planned their most audacious move yet. They wanted a radio. Messages were sent out via visitors. One day in the summer of 1994, a transistor radio (with earphones) was smuggled into Insein Prison in a bowl of unappetising, greasy rice. 'It was wonderful. We would listen at night. One person would listen and take notes, and when it was safe hand it to another person, so it wasn't in the same place. After that we began to publish our newsletter every day. We had purpose. We began to think of ourselves as useful people.'

Those days Win Tin would later recall as the best of his prison life. But in November 1995, rumour reached senior Insein officials of agitation in Block 3. The chief warden ordered that the prisoners be taken out and the cement floor drilled up. 'They thought we were hiding something,' said Win Tin. 'And we were.' In his cell was a squat-down, ceramic toilet bowl. One night he had pulled it out of the floor and under it hidden his precious, smuggled possessions: notes and letters from outside, books and a copy of *Newsweek* magazine. He had also hidden an iron rod that he had found in the exercise yard. To cover the broken surround around the toilet, Win Tin had mixed paper and water to make his own cement, and dried it to make a lid that he could remove when necessary to access his belongings. The search by senior wardens unearthed the stash, along with those of other prisoners, bringing an abrupt end to those golden days of plotting and smuggling, the committees and the newsletters, the political thrills that Win Tin craved.

Win Tin and twenty-four other inmates from Block 3 were sent to the Dog House as punishment. This was not a metaphorical designation; this was where the prison's Alsatian guard dogs were housed. 'Day and night we would listen to their barks and growls. It is a painful noise. When it's all you hear, it is a kind of a torture.' He could also hear the dogs being set on other prisoners. 'The dogs would be sent into the cell and the door locked. We could hear the growls of the dogs and the human screams.' This horror Win Tin was spared. But the months in the Dog House were punctuated by interrogations and beatings, and his isolation was strictly enforced. One of the worst experiences of his prison life came one December evening, on one of those rare nights in the year when it actually gets cold in Rangoon. A prison officer came to his cell and said he was to be taken for interrogation. He was hooded and handcuffed and led out into the chilly air. The interrogation room was occupied, and Win Tin was left outside, and then apparently forgotten. 'I was left there for the whole night, my hands behind my back. I was freezing and shivering. The hood was thick and soon I could hardly breathe, it was the same air inside. I was suffocating, I was freezing. I thought I was to die.'

After several dark months in the Dog House, Win Tin was returned to a normal wing. He and his co-conspirators in Block 3 had been handed fresh sentences totalling 177 years. The interrogations continued sporadically, depending on political events beyond the prison walls. What new information the solitary Win Tin could have been harbouring was not clear. But his main enemy throughout his remaining years in jail was tedium. The loneliness, the long silent days. 'Most of the time I had nothing to do. We were not allowed to read or write,' he said. 'I was in a small room, about ten feet by twelve. I remembered I read in a Van Gogh biography that while he was in an asylum he walked round and round. So I laid out my sleeping mat in the centre and would walk round and round. I would recite poems and religious texts. Day after day I did it. I never became depressed, because there was always tomorrow and tomorrow would be a new day.'

Small details became important. He would observe colonies of ants, their behaviour. He would leave out a small cube of sugar, and watch its discovery by an ant on reconnaissance. The ant would return to the group and inform them of his discovery. The ant army would then march back across the bare concrete floor, only to discover that

Win Tin had removed the sugar. 'They would not find any sugar at all. Then they would punish the ant. That was my small revenge against intelligence agents.' His cell had a metal gate opening to the outside, and he would spend hours observing the clouds, taking note of their changing patterns day by day, season by season. 'Watching the clouds, the beauty of the world, these things made me feel proud, and happy to be alive. I did not feel sorry for myself or sorry for the other prisoners like me. On the contrary, I felt we were living an exalted life.'

When in the yard for exercise, or on his way to see a fortnightly visitor, Win Tin would surreptitiously pick up a red brick, or piece of brick, and hide it in the folds of his *longyi*. On the floor of his cell he would start to grind it up. The task required patience. 'It was tedious work. I had to rub it hundreds of thousands of times over many days to grind it up.' He would put the powder in his tin cup, add a little water and then strain the reddish brown mixture through the cotton of his *longyi*. He was left with a fine paste, which he would leave in the hot sun to harden into a kind of a chalk. With this he could write. 'I would write poems. I wrote so many poems. When they were still fresh in my mind, I would recite some of them to my friends who visited me. They would memorise them and write them down. That way some of my poems survived.' Unsurprisingly, perhaps, Win Tin was also fascinated by the passage of time. He used his chalk to mark up calendars on his walls and would set himself challenges to calculate the day of the week on a date years ago. He would use his grasp of time to butter up the prison guards, most of whom had little education and only knew their date of birth in the Burmese calendar, but were supposed to know the equivalent date in the Western calendar for official forms and the like. He would help them out in the hope of a small favour in return.

✧ ✿ ✿ ✿ ✿ ✿ ✧

Shortly after daybreak on Tuesday 23 September 2008, a prison warden came to Win Tin's cell. In the preceding few months, the prisoners had been allowed a new morning privilege – coffee mix, a three-in-one sachet containing coffee, milk powder and sugar which is Burma's favourite hot beverage. The warden handed over a tin kettle of hot water for the coffee, and told Win Tin to pack his things; he would be released that day. With defences built up from previous disappointments, Win Tin refused to believe it. There had been false dawns before. He didn't have much to pack, just a couple of books on Buddhism and a clean shirt and *longyi*, all in prison blue. But he left his belongings where they were, sat on the floor in the middle of his cell and refused to move. There had been many times over the previous nineteen years when Win Tin could have secured his release. Insein's director general had offered him freedom on several occasions, but always with conditions. First, he would have to sign a 401 Form, in which the prisoner must promise not to undertake any political activities after release. If the bond was broken, the prisoner would have to serve the entire sentence again. 'I was first given the option to do this in 1991, and I said no,' said Win Tin. 'And from time to time after that they would ask me.' Many other political detainees signed that bond and were freed. Was that cowardly? 'Not really,' said Win Tin, with his consistent generosity. 'Some of them believed that prison life was useless, they wanted to be out to do work from the outside. So they did it not out of cowardice but out of their own reasoning. But I couldn't do it. I was a politician, a founder of the NLD and secretary of the party. If I did it then the government would make a big thing of it, publish it as propaganda. I could not let that happen.'

Throughout the day, official after official came to Win Tin's cell to try to persuade him to pack his things and prepare to leave. The elderly prisoner remained where he was, sitting cross-legged in the centre of the cell, refusing to move. The protest was a form of self-protection. Two years earlier, the release process had gone as far as a special ceremony in front of the director general in the prison's main hall. Win Tin was told he had been granted immediate, unconditional release. An hour later, without explanation, he was taken to his cell and locked up again. Nothing more was said. So on that Tuesday, Win Tin stayed put for the entire day, ignoring the increasingly frantic pleas of wardens to change into his clean set of clothes and prepare for release. At 4.30 p.m., the director general himself appeared. 'The DG came in and sat beside me. He assured me there would be no 401, I would be released without condition, and he had come to take me in his car to the main gate.' Win Tin relented, almost, agreeing to go with the director but refusing to change out of his dirty prison uniform. 'They told me if I did not get changed I would be charged with stealing state property. I think they were ashamed that people would see me like that. I said fine, you can charge me, because either I am leaving in these clothes or I will go out naked.' In the end it was the director who relented.

Win Tin sat next to the director general in the back of his black, chauffeur-driven SUV. They drove slowly along the elevated internal road that cut across the prison, looped round the central tower and led onwards to the main north gate. In two decades, this was the first time that Win Tin had seen these parts of the prison; when he had been moved around before, or taken to see visitors, he had always been hooded. They got out of the car and stepped into the director's office. Win Tin was served a glass of orange juice and the director assured him, once again, that there would be no 401 and no change of clothes. They agreed he would be taken to a friend's house, quite close to Insein. Win Tin breathed deeply, sipped his juice and began to believe it was actually happening.

They stepped out of the office to the car that would drive Win Tin to freedom. As he approached the car door someone took a photograph with a flash. Win Tin swung around, surprised: photography was banned inside the prison grounds. 'I looked and saw it was a girl. She took some more pictures and then started to ask questions: "How do you feel about being released? Do you feel happy?" The questions were impertinent. I was so disturbed and annoyed I said many harsh words about the government. I said prison life was hell, and the whole of Burma was a prison, so I had no reason to be joyful about being released.' If Win Tin had allowed himself a few brief moments of happy anticipation, they were quickly over. He was back on message. The young female journalist, brought into the prison to prepare a special puff piece, slunk away, ashamed. The next day her father came to the house where Win Tin was staying to apologise. 'I told him I didn't like those questions, so impertinent, as if I had something to celebrate.' The father had bowed his head. 'I know, I know,' he said.

At 5.50 p.m., just minutes before it grew dark, seventy-eight-year-old Win Tin was released from Insein Prison. They had planned to drive him out of the main gate, but so many journalists had gathered that they changed plan at the last minute and drove him out along a side route through the dingy houses and washing lines of the prison guards' family quarters. He was dropped at the house of his friend and immediately mobbed by the waiting media and many of his old friends from journalism and politics. He did a string of interviews, for the Democratic Voice of Burma, Voice of America, Radio Free Asia and the BBC Burmese Service. He was amazed to see himself beamed back on satellite television, and to hear his voice on the Burmese radio broadcasts throughout the evening. His release, part of an amnesty of prisoners on that day, also merited a few paragraphs in the international media. 'Although exiled dissidents welcomed the release of Win Tin and the others, they dismissed it as a cynical ploy by the junta to defuse tensions as world leaders gather for the UN summit in New York amid calls for even tougher sanctions,' read a piece in the *Guardian*. Win Tin also played down the significance of his release when more than two thousand other Burmese prisoners of conscience remained behind bars: 'I could not be happy when my colleagues were still in jail and the rest of the country was one big, open-air prison.' But while the strength of his convictions had always overpowered his worldly needs, he could not help but surrender to the enjoyment of his first evening with friends for two decades. 'On a personal level, I was happy to be surrounded by friends, especially because my friends are really my family. In prison I could only talk to visitors by telephone, through a thick window. Now I could reach out and touch them,' he smiled gently. One of his best friends, Ludu Sein Win, a well-known journalist and writer who had been sent to prison on the Coco Islands and tortured many times, was carried into the living room, his oxygen tank in tow. After a blink of shock at how the other had aged, the two men fell deep into conversation. The women had prepared a special dish of *ohn no kauk swe*, coconut chicken noodles, but Win Tin barely touched them.

Food would become the abiding reminder of the privations of prison. 'I cannot digest, I will never be able to. Even now, I can only eat very little,' Win Tin told me. After a few years to reflect on his long incarceration, had he forgiven his captors? I tossed out the question casually as we neared the end of our interviews, almost as an afterthought, imagining I knew well what the answer would be. This kind, radiant old man, Burma's longest serving political prisoner, so similar in his manner to Nelson Mandela, sharing a life story of resistance and endurance – surely he would smile serenely, tell me he bore no grudge. His watery eyes held mine. 'I cannot forgive,' he said firmly. 'Although I am not a vengeful person I cannot clean the slate completely. I cannot do it. But I do not think or dream about it. I have left it. I am not going back to the past.'

# 9
# The Lady

We could look across Inya Lake to Aung San Suu Kyi's house from J's Bistro, popular with expatriates for coffee or Sunday brunch with its cooling fans, rattan furniture and cushions covered in Burmese cotton. There were little brass bells on the tables to summon the waiters, a table stacked with old copies of *Vogue* and *Vanity Fair* as well as colouring books and jars of felt tips for the children. The large French windows opened on to a wooden deck on the north side of the lake, lined with plants in terracotta pots. It was a good place to take visitors, for whom catching a glimpse of 'The Lady's' house, and even snatching a zoomed-in, blurry photograph was an essential component of their Rangoon itinerary. Waiting for our coffees, we would saunter out on to the deck, feigning an interest in the cormorants and herons that swooped low over the silvery water. There, on the far side of the lake, was the once grand but now mouldering white-painted house, with a sloping lawn running down to the water's edge. Sometimes I took some pocket-sized binoculars to sneak a closer look, but only once saw any activity in Suu Kyi's back garden – two workmen had shinned up a coconut tree to cut back its upper fronds, supervised, I guessed, by one of Suu Kyi's two housemaids, who looked up from the grass but was not the slender figure that I knew Suu Kyi to be. I never once saw any sign of *her*, by then the world's most famous political prisoner, a woman admired the world over for her self-sacrificing, principled resistance to Burma's military regime. She was so near (her house was just half a mile from ours) but so far away, under house arrest for the best part of two decades in what had been her mother's home on University Avenue. Armed police manned roadblocks on the street in front of the house, while at the back, the lake had an unmarked but well-observed 'exclusion zone', across which rowers and canoeists were warned not to cross.

In May 2009 came the first whiff of a bizarre story concerning Suu Kyi – and the lake. The state-run newspaper the *New Light of Myanmar* reported that an American man had been arrested while swimming, at night, away from Suu Kyi's house. It emerged that fifty-three-year-old John Yettaw, a devout Mormon who had fashioned his own homemade wooden flippers for the swim, had spent two nights in the home of Suu Kyi, who, under the terms of her house arrest was not allowed any guests unless sanctioned by the authorities. Suu Kyi had begged him to leave, but had felt obliged to offer him hospitality when he pleaded exhaustion. As a matter of principle, she later said, she did not report his presence to the security guards in front of her house. The motivation for Yettaw's escapade was unclear; his family in Missouri said he was mentally ill and they were unaware that he had even travelled to Asia. As far as Suu Kyi was concerned, the middle-aged American was an unwelcome guest, and her aides said she had only allowed him to stay because he complained of feeling unwell. Speculation swirled on the Internet. What was behind it all? Was he a CIA spy? Or a regime stooge? As odd as it seemed, many people believed the latter, that Yettaw was sent to mess things up for Suu Kyi just as her term of detention was about to expire and there was the possibility that she would at last be freed. In fact, the most accurate description of Yettaw was probably an 'eccentric' – he acted alone, believing he was on a mission to save Suu Kyi. But his antics were a gift to the military authorities, who, true to form, arrested her at her home and put her on trial for breaching the terms of her house arrest.

For a few days during the monsoon season of 2009, a fleet of limousines and four-wheel drives with diplomatic plates cruised up the rain-soaked Insein Road each morning, whipping up arcs of spray that soaked the sidewalks and slippered feet of pedestrians. The convoy was heading north to the prison where Suu Kyi's trial was held in a special court. Foreign diplomats had been given permission to attend, giving the outside world the first chance in years to catch a glimpse of the delicate, composed woman who, even in the most difficult of circumstances, always managed to find a fresh flower to wear in her hair. 'She seemed to crackle with energy,' said British ambassador Mark Canning, who sat in on the trial. The Philippines chargé d'affaires, Joselito Chad Jacinto, was equally charmed. 'She exuded an aura which can only be described as awe-inspiring,' he enthused. Suu Kyi was not allowed to approach the benches where the diplomats from Britain, Australia and Asian nations were seated, but she rewarded their daily attendance with a gracious smile and called out to them in English: 'I hope to meet you again in better times.' The thirteen-week trial was dismissed as a sham, Suu Kyi was convicted and another eighteen months were added to her sentence. Those 'better times' she had referred to seemed a remote, unlikely prospect. I never expected that I would meet Aung San Suu Kyi. Neither did I anticipate the dramatic political changes that were to follow, and nor did anyone else.

❧ ✿ ✿ ✿ ✿ ✿ ❧

The barrier breached, we surged forward, past the sign saying 'Restricted Area'. An uncertain pause then, as if we expected to be stopped, but no, the police had stepped to the side of the road, watching, smiling even, their guns slung casually over their shoulders. Incredulous at our freedom, we sped to a trot, then a full-on gallop, the joy of the moment manifested in laughter, little leaps, and punches into the warm, twilight air. The eighteen months had passed, and we were racing towards Aung San Suu Kyi's house, because (although we didn't yet completely believe it) it appeared that the Lady had just been released from her latest stint of house arrest. Two hundred yards down University Avenue, on the right, was the house, a tatty fence, grey metal gate, the red sign of her National League for Democracy party, and above that a rain-battered portrait of her heroic father, General Aung San. I had joined the crowd of hundreds of Suu Kyi supporters who had thrown off their fear to come to see their heroine. They thronged around her gate, holding aloft portraits of their leader, some with little playing card-sized pictures they may have kept hidden in their pockets for years. The crowd pulsed with excitement. 'Long Live Aung San Suu Kyi!' Our eyes were fixed on the gate. Suddenly there she was, standing before us, beaming at us. We leapt into the air, as one. '*Amay Suu, Amay Suu!*' 'Mother Suu! Mother Suu!' the crowd screamed.

It was 13 November 2010 when Aung San Suu Kyi emerged from seven years of house arrest, radiant and calm, as if she had never doubted this day would come. After a day of speculation as to whether she would actually be set free even though her sentence had reached its end, in the late afternoon the police had suddenly removed the barriers on University Avenue. Moments later she was there, standing at her fence in a lilac jacket with, of course, the customary flowers in her hair. Her head and shoulders were above the metal spikes of the gate; presumably she was standing on a stool or ladder behind it. Fleetingly, her hand reached up to smooth her swept-up hair. She smiled and nodded, and made a victory sign with her right hand. Minutes passed; the crowd was torn between yelling her name and wanting to hear her voice. Her fingers touched her lips, and there was quiet. 'There is a time for silence and a time for talking,' she told her supporters. 'We will work together, united. Only then can we achieve our goal.' Mobile phones were held up to click photographs, and flashes of light danced like fireflies as darkness fell. The sight of the cell phones, Suu Kyi said later, was new to her; she had never spoken into a mobile and didn't realise they could take pictures too. Next to me were two men, sweating and elated, clutching their postcard-sized Suu Kyi portraits. 'Very happy, very happy!' they shouted above the din.

It was all that needed to be said. Suu Kyi's freedom brought pure joy, a visceral reaction to the righting of a wrong, and excitement that this inspirational leader would again be able to guide her supporters, plan policies with party colleagues and enjoy some simple pleasures that had been denied to her for so long, like speaking by telephone to her two sons. But while joy was unbounded, expectations were not. The release of Suu Kyi came six days after the government had held Burma's first elections for twenty years, an event that had brought not optimism, but more a sense that the army was just looking for new ways to hold on to power. Under the new constitution pushed through in 2008, the military would hold 25 per cent of the seats in the new parliament in Naypyidaw, and the vote itself was blatantly rigged in favour of the army's proxy, the Union Solidarity and Development Party, which scooped up the bulk of the remaining seats. There was reason to be wary. This was the third time that Suu Kyi had been freed after a total of fifteen years of detention spanning more than two decades. On previous occasions, the junta had fairly quickly found reason to re-arrest her. In 2003, when she had been free for just a year, Suu Kyi's convoy was attacked by a government-hired mob at a rally in the central Burmese town of Depayin and more than seventy of her supporters were killed. The authorities detained her again 'for her own protection'. So hope was tempered with realism. For all the excitement of that day in November, few Burmese people, after so many years of disappointment, dared to dream of a better future. 'We feel powerless now, more than ever,' Ma Thida, a health worker who I had met through my NGO work, told me. 'The government is releasing her because they think they have won the election and can control her and the country completely. How can she do anything?'

≈ ✿ ✿ ✿ ✿ ✿ ≈

The next day, a Sunday, Suu Kyi addressed her supporters again, this time from the balcony of the NLD headquarters under the gleaming stupa of Shwedagon Pagoda. She had told us, in her no-nonsense, schoolmistressy manner, to be there at twelve o'clock sharp. But this was Burma, where things do not run like clockwork. By midday, the crowd was still swelling chaotically on the Shwegondine Road. It sprawled across the street and up the grassy bank on the other side. At first cars were crawling through the mass of people, slowly, politely, with no beeping – as is the Burmese way – but then the pressure of newcomers from both ends grew too strong, and the people were packed in too tightly to move even if they had wanted to. There was one person who had to get through, though, and at about quarter past (late herself) Suu Kyi arrived in the obligatory beaten-up Toyota Corolla, which squeezed to within ten metres of the building before her security detail – a dozen burly boys wearing white Aung San Suu Kyi T-shirts – formed a ring around her and virtually carried her inside. A football stadium roar went up. One of the NLD 'uncles', the senior party members who had tried, with limited success, to keep the party on course while their leader was imprisoned, came out to the platform set up at the front of the two-storey building and urged us to be quiet, and to sit, before the Lady would address us. Sit? It seemed impossible. Our backsides would take up a lot more ground space than our two feet. But these were orders and this was a compliant, eager crowd. So down we all went, holding on to the shoulders in front of us and finding ourselves in great intimacy with our neighbours, bottoms and laps concertinaed. By mid-November, the ferocious strength of the Burmese sun should have begun to wane, ready for the comfortable winter months of December and January. But on that clear day, the sun beat down on us with force, and sweat streamed down happy, expectant faces.

When Suu Kyi emerged, in daylight this time, I could feel around me the desperate, searching hope channelled into this one woman, and wondered at the pressure she must have felt. But if she felt it, she did not betray it. Her voice clear and warm, her speech unscripted, she spoke of her hope for a new, democratic Burma. 'You must go away and eat a lot of rice, to give you strength for the struggle ahead!' she told the masses crammed before her. 'None of us can do it alone. We must work together.' It was clear Suu Kyi had lost none of her famous charisma. She somehow managed to single out individuals among the sea of faces for a look or a smile. In one extraordinary moment, she locked eyes with a young, bare-chested activist in the heart of the crowd who raised a clenched, tattooed fist in return. Also among us were secret service agents, poorly disguised with their neat, side-parted hair and darting eyes. Everyone knew who they were and everyone ignored them. No one cared. As before in Burma, I felt the strength of the collective, the power and fearlessness that solidarity can bring. Yet beneath all the excitement, it did not seem cynical to regard Suu Kyi's release as a gimmick, a PR stunt on the part of the regime. More than two thousand political prisoners remained behind bars, the government had just presided over a fraudulent election, and the septuagenarian Than Shwe remained in power. What had really changed? The person most able to answer that question, the one who had truly seen it all before, was the Lady herself.

✥ ✿ ✿ ✿ ✿ ✿ ✥

I paced around the garden, the only place I could get a signal, yelling into the cheap, Chinese mobile phone. It had a little telescopic aerial that I had just pulled up in case it helped. This was a phone that supposedly could not be traced back to me. It contained a $50 SIM card that gave me a measly number of call minutes, after which I had to throw the SIM card away and buy another one – with a new telephone number. My regular phone was rented from a Burmese friend – a common way of avoiding the arcane bureaucracy of acquiring a mobile – and I didn't want to land her in trouble by using it to call the NLD's number. It was at least my sixth call of the day to them; I was running down my credit in my quest to secure the hottest ticket in town – an interview with the newly released Aung San Suu Kyi. The man acting as Suu Kyi's gatekeeper, the NLD party spokesman Nyan Win, I knew well, having met and interviewed him already. I tried to play up my credentials as a Rangoon-based journalist (I didn't keep that a secret from the NLD, they were the dissidents after all, but I always went by my pseudonym, just to be on the safe side). I hoped my record of reporting on the NLD's struggles would push me up the list. It was hard to say. Nyan Win, a government attorney before he joined the democracy movement, started off the week his usual even-handed, inscrutable self, but became more and more stressed under persistent pressure from the gang of foreign journalists who had sneaked into Burma to cover the dramatic events and were now desperate for their moment with the Lady. He hung up on me a few times, but I couldn't blame him. Nyan Win was an erudite, softly spoken lawyer, not a spin doctor, and I often wondered after that whether part of him yearned for the days of blissful isolation when Suu Kyi was imprisoned and the press rarely bothered him.

On Wednesday, four days after Suu Kyi's release, I phoned Nyan Win for about the twenty-eighth time. Expecting another brush off, I was dumbstruck to be told the Lady would see me the next day. I was to come to the NLD's headquarters at two o'clock. (Of course I would rather have met her in the house where she had spent all her years in detention, but it was clear that the terms of this interview were not up for negotiation.) I would get thirty minutes with her. My heart raced as I sat down to write out my questions. I emailed the *Independent's* foreign desk. I thought through some contingencies in case I was followed by the MI agents stationed across the road from her office. I took a taxi into town to buy some more phone credit. On Anawrahta Street, where there was a cluster of Indian-run stores selling cameras, laptops and mobile phones, I walked past a little shop called Face, painted white, pristine and minimalist, and strangely out of place in Rangoon's grimy city centre. It sold beautifully packaged creams and lotions arranged on glass shelves. I had been thinking of taking Suu Kyi a gift – a departure from the usual journalistic code of ethics, but this seemed to be a special circumstance. Some expensive body lotion, lavender-scented hand cream, surely these little luxuries had been denied to her over all these years? I knew from reading about Suu Kyi that even democracy icons were not immune to vanity and she clearly enjoyed looking after her appearance. On the occasions that she had been allowed visitors under house arrest she had requested not only books – which she loved – but also Max Factor lipstick and mascara. I went inside and bought her a gift set, wrapped beautifully in a white box tied up with a purple ribbon.

I arrived for my appointment two hours early, in sunglasses and a baseball cap, like a celebrity trying to avoid the attentions of the paparazzi. My trusted taxi driver Kyaw Swar had zipped right up to the gates of the NLD office and I hoped the eye-watering glare of the midday sun had obscured my hurried entry. In a small rucksack I had a spare set of clothes, and my plan, if I was followed after the interview, was to take a taxi to the British embassy in the hope I would be mistaken for a diplomat. I would go to the busy library there, change in the ladies' and emerge a few hours later, hopefully looking different. My scheme didn't sound very sophisticated, but the MI agents hadn't impressed me with their competence so far. On the other hand, I knew journalists who had been detained and deported having been identified for movements considerably less incriminating than visiting the NLD office. And if I, as a Rangoon resident, was caught it would be a lot more serious – I would implicate those around me and in particular my husband's aid organisation. I hadn't said anything to him about it the evening before. I knew he would worry if I told him about the interview, so I had decided to wait until it was over – easier to ask for forgiveness than permission, I told myself.

Like Sleeping Beauty's castle, the party's chaotic headquarters had come to life again after many years. During Suu Kyi's incarceration, party members only opened the office for meetings on national holidays. Now it was buzzing with activity: well-dressed ladies sat behind a trestle table selling hastily produced Aung San Suu Kyi memorabilia, another woman stirred a vat of curry by the door. Opposition activists, invigorated by their leader's release, sat in small groups, their hands waving about as they discussed policy and the future. One man armed with a roll of tape busied himself covering every available space left on the pale green, mildewed walls with newly printed posters of the Lady. To my disappointment, I saw that I was not the first journalist to arrive. Other foreigners were standing against the filing cabinets, sweaty and silent. At first, there was tension among us, the usual camaraderie between journalists replaced by suspicion and competitiveness. No one wanted to talk. Instead I chatted to Peter, an NLD volunteer, who had taken on the job of signing us all in. Now twenty-seven, he was the son of a political prisoner and had joined the NLD as soon as he was old enough. While devoted to the cause, his membership of the outlawed opposition movement was causing him serious personal problems, he told me. He couldn't get a girlfriend. Well educated, not badly off and certainly good-looking, his political activities made him just too risky to hang out with. He looked across the crowded room at two slender young women in tightly wrapped sarongs who were laying out tin cups by the water dispenser. 'But maybe I will find one here,' he grinned.

I was third on the list behind the Associated Press and a reporter and photographer from *El Pais*. We all kept asking Peter to repeat the running order and to tell us again how long we would have. We needed the reassurance. If these were the first media interviews the Lady was giving, we just had to see her that day. I looked at the young, male cameraman opposite me – unwashed, unshaven, and looking like he had slept in his jeans and T-shirt – and wondered whether he thought this was appropriate attire to meet the ever-immaculate Lady. I had at least worn a skirt and made an effort to look smart, but we had all by now succumbed to the intense, humid heat. Clicking our digital recorders on and off, we looked feverish and slightly deranged, our hair plastered down on our heads. Two men arrived to install a new fridge at the bottom of the stairs. Straining for its metaphorical significance, we all took frantic notes.

There was a commotion at the open door and I realised that at last she was here. The crowd parted to make way, and she stopped only to bow her head and clasp the elderly hand of a shaven-headed Buddhist nun. Then she swept past and up the enclosed wooden staircase to her 'sitting room', which Peter had told me had been hastily cleaned, painted and carpeted the day after her release. The first batches of journalists were called up, and then, after another hour or two of waiting, I was finally summoned up the stairs to the holding area outside her office door. Dry-mouthed, I sat on a rickety fold-down chair and contemplated the peeling paint and bare concrete floor. I fiddled with my damp, flat hair. I could hear the wail of a baby from the shop next door. Then the door opened to the light-filled room, and there was the Lady, shaking the hands of the reporters in the group before me. I removed my shoes (as is the Burmese custom) and stepped inside. 'No, no, not there, sit down here next to me,' she commanded, warm and bossy at the same time. Suu Kyi told me she had hardly had time to breathe since her release five days earlier. I knew she had many more pressing matters on her mind, but for half an hour she fixed her full attention on me.

❧ ✿ ✿ ✿ ✿ ✿ ❧

She sat straight backed, of course, in a fitted grey blouse and long silk *tamein*, her hair pulled back in a ring of tiny yellow roses. Where to begin? Worried about the constraint of time, I made the mistake of ploughing through my list of questions, some of which others at the paper had sent for me to ask. We skipped too quickly from her routine in detention to her policy on sanctions to the recent elections. I jumped around topics instead of following up on the things that really interested me – her feelings about being separated from her family, and her ambitions now she was free. My approach suited her down to the ground. Suu Kyi did not want to get into the intricacies of her personal life; no journalist has really managed to crack the invisible, protective wall she has built around herself. She batted away questions that sought to delve into her feelings about the sacrifices she had made, the missing years with her family. Compared to Burma's thousands of other political prisoners, flung into squalid jails across the country, detention in a lakeside villa wasn't so bad, she tried to argue. 'It embarrasses me to talk about the personal cost to me when I see what other political prisoners have to put up with,' she said. 'Whatever I have had to undergo is nothing. Of course, one always thinks that one's family is lovelier than every other family in the world. That's only natural.'

Suu Kyi spent much of her early life abroad with her diplomat mother after her father's assassination when she was aged just two. As a student in England, she met her future husband, the academic Michael Aris, and settled down with him on a street of substantial terraced houses in north Oxford. The couple had two sons, Alexander and Kim, and visitors to the Aris family home recall a noisy household, full of laughter and the exotic smells of Suu Kyi's Burmese cooking. 'It was a normal family life with a father and a mother and children and a house and a dog,' Suu Kyi told me, matter-of-factly. 'We had normal friends; whatever we did seems very normal in comparison with what I'm doing now.' In the spring of 1988 (when her sons were fifteen and eleven), Suu Kyi was called back to Burma to care for her dying mother. It was a visit that would change the course of her life. She arrived at a time of political unrest – students, office workers and monks had taken to the streets in protest at the oppressions of military rule. 'I didn't consciously choose politics over my family, I just chose to get involved,' she explained. 'At that time, in 1988, there was this tremendous upsurge of people power, and everybody for a short time was involved in the uprising, and I just thought of it as a citizen's duty to be part of the movement.' This was new territory for everyone, and she could not have guessed at the personal toll it would take. But once she had dipped her toe into Burmese politics, there was no going back.

On 26 August, Suu Kyi made her first public speech, beneath Shwedagon, and half a million people braved the monsoon rain and mud to hear her. The crowd was struck by her extraordinary charisma, determination and her resemblance to her father. Overnight, she became the democracy movement's leader. The military rulers felt intensely threatened by this wisp-like, passionate woman and in less than a year, the newly established State Law and Order Restoration Council (SLORC) ordered that she be placed under house arrest. That was the start of what would be a total of fifteen years of incarceration in her mother's decaying villa. 'They put barricades on our street on both sides of my house. The chairman of the Township Law and Order Committee came to my house with lots of other people and read out the detention order placing me under house arrest. That was it. Then they searched my house from top to bottom.'

Suu Kyi recalled the crushing sense of being completely alone. Security agents were camped in her lakeside garden, among its blooms of frangipani and jasmine. Her phone line was cut; she had no television, no computer. Just a radio. 'I was alone in the house and all the security people were camped in the garden. In *my* garden. And apart from the times when my family was allowed to visit me I hardly saw anybody from the outside,' she said. 'The first years were the worst. They threw me into the deep end. And after that I could swim beautifully.' She smiled wryly.

Her husband Michael had returned to Oxford with the boys, but during her first stint of house arrest they were allowed to visit during the school summer holidays. The last visa was granted in the monsoon season of 1995. Michael Aris later wrote that those days he spent with his wife at the tropical lakeside house were 'among my happiest memories of our many years of marriage. It was wonderfully peaceful... I did not suspect this would be the last time we would be together for the foreseeable future.' In fact, it was the very last time. Two years later, he was diagnosed with prostate cancer. The Burmese authorities denied him permission to visit his wife again, and Suu Kyi made the painful decision not to travel to England, knowing that if she did she would never be allowed to return to her homeland. Michael Aris died on his fifty-third birthday, in 1999. 'My family accepted that I could not go back, and they understood. I don't think they were happy about it, but neither was I,' Suu Kyi told me. 'But I was never in doubt about what I should do, and neither was my husband.'

During the seven years of her last detention, the authorities delivered to her just one letter from each of her sons, by then in their late twenties and thirties. Suu Kyi relied on 'inner resources' and a strict daily routine. She rose each day at 4.30 a.m. for early morning meditation. Each day was devoted to what she regarded as work, listening to the radio, making sure she was up to date with news. Losing touch was what she feared most. 'If I missed something, there was no one to say, "Did you hear about that?" So I had to listen to everything. That was my job.' She read avidly, and played her out-of-tune piano.

From this peaceful solitude she had been thrown, overnight, into a maelstrom of constant company and constant demands. She was tired, but unwilling to slow down, worried as she was that her freedom could be short-lived. She had talked by phone to Barack Obama and David Cameron; she had held meetings with the senior brass of her party, trying to move the stagnant democracy movement forward. That was her one aim, she said: democracy and nothing less. Of course, at that time, Suu Kyi didn't know what her freedom really meant; after all, she had been there before, only to be locked up again. She was still distrustful of the generals, and dismissive of the recent elections they had held. Why had she been freed? Her guess was as good as ours. 'I think they had simply run out of excuses to keep me locked up,' she said. In fact it was more calculated than that. Her release turned out to be the beginning of a controlled evolution by the generals that steered Burma towards a political transition while avoiding violent regime change, shielding the senior generals from retribution for their injustices. At that time, though, Suu Kyi just knew that her release had generated a burst of energy, and she was desperate to harness it. 'There are so many young people who support us, full of energy and vigour and vim. But they have to learn not to be afraid of political contacts and politics. They need to have courage.'

Her aide knocked on the door to signal our time was up. I gathered up my notebook and tape recorder, and remembered the gift I had for her in my rucksack. Sheepishly I took out the white, ribboned box and put it in front of her on the wooden coffee table. 'I just thought, well, you might have missed things like this,' I said. She smiled a brilliant smile. 'Oh thank you! That is terribly kind. You know, after all these years, I've realised that kindness is the thing I appreciate the most.' She ushered me to the door.

☙ ✿✿✿✿✿ ❧

I next saw Aung San Suu Kyi a week later at Rangoon airport. Her younger son Kim had been granted a visa in Bangkok and was on the first flight. The wires had reported his departure from Thailand so I jumped in Kyaw Swar's taxi and we raced to the airport as fast as the Toyota Sprinter would carry us. When I arrived she was already there, at first standing in the arrivals hall with all the other families who had come to greet the early morning flights. But then Suu Kyi, a celebrity even to the servants of the military regime, was approached by an airport security officer and escorted through customs, past the baggage carousel, to a seat next to the passport counters. We could see her through the glass wall, sitting very still on the bench, her back to us. For the thirty minutes that she waited, her hands in her lap, she was not Burma's democracy leader, nor a prize-winning dissident. She was simply a mother, waiting to be reunited with the son she had not seen for a decade. When she spotted thirty-three-year-old Kim skipping down the steps from the airline gates, she stood up, smiling. She couldn't take her eyes off him as he queued to clear immigration. He bounded towards her and greeted her with a quick hug. She held his arms and stepped back to look properly at her son, almost a foot taller than her. When he took off his jacket to show her a tattoo of a peacock on his upper arm – the symbol of her National League for Democracy – she laughed.

Kim Aris had become the father of two children since he last saw his mother, but on that day he looked very much like a son – in a scruffy khaki T-shirt and jeans, a rucksack on his shoulders. His mother, by contrast, looked typically elegant, dressed in pale green silk. It occurred to me that his outfit may have been more thoughtfully chosen than it appeared to be. Emblazoned on his T-shirt was one of the monsters from the classic children's book *Where The Wild Things Are*. Perhaps Kim wanted to remind his mother of the family life they used to share in Oxford, or perhaps he just wanted to make her laugh.

It was hard to imagine the separation they had endured. Many around me had tears in their eyes; some looked away, so as not to intrude on this very personal family scene. But Suu Kyi did not cry. She threaded her arm through her son's and looked up at his fine-featured face, so similar to hers, and beamed.

# 10
# Written in the Stars

On an airless Sunday morning, I was sitting on a wooden chair next to an open window with my right hand upturned on the table in front of me. Min Wai had grasped my fingers tightly, and, with a magnifying glass to his eye, had bent his head low over my palm. There was a long silence before he spoke and I was suddenly worried about what he was going to say. Min Wai lit a cigarette and exhaled towards the open window, but the smoke hung like a cloud in the still air. I looked at him expectantly. He smiled. I need not have worried. The lines on my palm foretold only good things. My health was good and would remain so. In my mid-forties, I would enjoy great success and riches, followed, twenty years later, by overwhelming, unprecedented, astounding success. My visit to the palm reader was going well.

One of the easier ways to go about being an undercover journalist, I had discovered, was to do the ordinary, touristy things that the Burmese would expect foreigners to do anyway. A visit to Rangoon's fetid zoo, a trishaw ride around the colonial downtown, or a tour of a pagoda were unlikely to attract undue attention, but could give me an ear on the city's background chatter. Conversations with the elephant keeper, my favourite *saiq-ka* driver (the octogenarian Mr Coconut) or a Buddhist monk keen to practise his English, while not startling in isolation, could be pieced together to build a truer picture of Burmese life. I liked to think of it as work, and my visit to one of Rangoon's most celebrated palm readers was part of the same exercise.

The Burmese are fascinated by palmistry, astrology, numerology and fortune telling of any kind. The vast majority of the Burmese population are Buddhist, but many mix their practice of Theravada Buddhism with the worship of *nats*, or spirits, and an array of superstitious beliefs including the interpretation of planetary movements or earthly phenomena to predict the future and explain the past. Great store is set by astrological readings in determining the correct dates for weddings, funerals and other important events, and wealthy Burmese women may even book in their Caesarean sections on auspicious dates.

In Burmese history, superstition has been a constant and powerful force. In the nineteenth century, the demise of King Thibaw's white elephant, a species revered as a symbol of power and good fortune (the elephant lived in extravagant surroundings, adorned with diamonds and fed from a gold trough), was regarded as an unpropitious omen, and was soon followed by the monarch's ousting by British colonisers. At Burma's independence in 1948, the exact timing of the handover of power – 4.20 in the morning on 4 January – was decided after intense consultations with the country's leading soothsayers. In 1987, General Ne Win introduced the unconventional kyat denominations of forty-five and ninety, having decided that the value of the notes had to be divisible by his lucky number, nine.

In more recent history, the wrath of Cyclone Nargis unleashed countless prophesies, including the imminent downfall of the military regime, a prediction that turned out to have substance. And on one memorable, clear Burmese night in March 2009, the crescent moon, which in the northern tropics sits upturned like a bowl, was joined in the black sky by two bright stars above it, creating a celestial smiley face. The wondrous sight drew awestruck families out of their houses and sparked a frenzy of positive omens.

☙ ✿ ✿ ✿ ✿ ✿ ❧

Min Wai saw clients seven days a week in his dishevelled wooden house in the northern Rangoon suburb of Okkalapa, and charged 4,000 kyats (about four dollars) for a half- hour reading. By Burmese standards he was pretty well off. His two-storey house had several bedrooms and a well-equipped kitchen with a gas-burning stove. On the carpeted floor of his living room sat three voltage regulators, devices bought by those who could afford them to tame the city's erratic electricity supply and to prevent sudden power surges from blowing up appliances such as DVD players or rice cookers, a common and frustrating occurrence in Rangoon households. In a white T-shirt and sarong, Min Wai was sitting on a plastic chair at his desk, with a powerful anglepoise lamp, a glass ashtray and three magnifying glasses set before him. On the wall behind him were several posters of the Lord Buddha and a framed black-and-white photograph of his wife, taken just before their wedding, a beautiful woman with her hair pinned up with flowers, gazing intently at the camera. She had died thirty years earlier.

On 2 March 1962, Min Wai graduated from teacher training college in Mandalay. At dawn the same day, tanks rolled into Rangoon and soldiers seized Prime Minister U Nu and senior government ministers from their beds and took them into custody. This was the *coup d'état* that would launch half a century of dictatorial rule. The instigator of the coup, army chief General Ne Win, installed himself as head of the Revolutionary Council. Like many of Burma's leaders before him, he was a superstitious man, fascinated by palmistry, astrology and numerology. Up in Mandalay, Min Wai was already deeply immersed in the teachings of the renowned Irish palmist Cheiro and had begun to meet practitioners in the Ponnar Kone quarter of the city. There he had befriended the great-grandchildren of Rama, the palmist of King Mindon, Thibaw's father. In exchange for knowledge of Cheiro's art of reading the lines of the hand, Rama's descendants taught the young teacher their ancient Indian technique, focusing on the palm's ridges.

After his graduation, Min Wai taught in a primary school by day, and read palms in the evening. Within a few years his client base had expanded hugely, to the extent that he had a waiting list for appointments. He decided to quit his teaching position and concentrate full time on palm reading and astrological interpretations. One of his early clients in Mandalay was Ni Ni Myint, a young history student living in a university dorm. 'When I told her she would become a queen, she was very excited,' Min Wai said. 'She kept coming back to see me.' In the early 1970s, true to the prediction, Ni Ni Myint married the dictator Ne Win, becoming his fourth wife and Burma's first lady. Min Wai became an indispensible member of her entourage and relocated with her to Rangoon.

A decade later, Ni Ni Myint, by now a respected history professor as well as the president's consort, arrived at Min Wai's house in a state of high excitement, bringing with her a fragment of a dream recalled by her husband. As the economic disaster wrought by Ne Win's ill-conceived 'Burmese Way to Socialism' had unfolded, the general's reaction had not been to cede governance to a more competent, civilian administration, but to blunder on, ruthlessly eliminating dissent along the way. The night before his wife visited the fortune teller, Ne Win had had an unusual dream. He had dreamt of a pagoda in which the *hti*, the gem-encrusted umbrella that sits at the tip of the spire, was double layered. 'It took me a while to interpret that dream. It was very unusual, and I knew it was very significant,' said Min Wai. 'I contemplated its meaning, I referred to many teachings. Then I saw the meaning. I told Ni Ni Myint that General San Yu would become president in Ne Win's place, but Ne Win would stay in power, he would have control from behind the throne. And that is exactly what happened.'

In this tense, backbiting atmosphere, several of the most powerful generals in the Burmese junta turned to Win Mai for consultations about their future. One of his most notable clients was Prime Minister Khin Nyunt, the feared military intelligence chief and the mastermind of Burma's web of spies who kept the nation under suffocating surveillance. Like most of the senior generals, Khin Nyunt was highly superstitious. For luck, he kept a white elephant, captured in the jungles of Arakan, dressed in royal regalia at his private temple near Rangoon's airport. Did Min Wai feel intimidated? 'I was honest,' he said. 'I just told him what I saw. And I was correct. All my readings were correct. I still have records. I predicted that he would be ousted, and he was.' In 2004, the junta's strongman Than Shwe decided that the rising power of Khin Nyunt had become a threat to his authority. The prime minister was arrested and his military intelligence network dismantled. Khin Nyunt spent more than seven years under house arrest at his home in Rangoon's Mingaladon district. The purge was good news for Burmese dissidents, and for people like me, trying to stay under the regime's radar. The wounded MI unit limped on, but was never the same slick, all-pervasive operation that it had been under Khin Nyunt.

Allowing himself to become so intimately entangled in the underhand dealings of Burmese politics in the dark days of the military's rule must have held dangers for the palm reader. Many of those close to the regime, who for one reason or another fell out of favour, found themselves imprisoned and wiped from the official memory. But Min Wai never felt the need for caution. Jail was not his destiny, he was sure of it. 'I have never been afraid,' he told me. 'Not of politicians or leaders, soldiers or anyone. My palm doesn't say that I will be arrested and I have faith in that.'

Min Wai developed the tact necessary for delivering unwelcome news. 'I never tell someone he will lose his power, rather I say their luck has run out or going forward will be difficult. I never tell a woman that she will become a widow. I tell her your husband will die before you. It's the same thing but it sounds softer. I have to be tactful with the words I use.' A few days earlier, Min Wai had had a consultation with a couple from Mandalay, a man of about fifty and his wife who was around thirty-five. 'When they married, he told her he was single. Together they had three children,' the palm reader said. 'But actually he has nine children and two other wives. From her side, he has three children but from his side he has nine children. I can see all this in his palm. If I tell the wife the truth, they will fight. Sometimes I decide to keep things to myself.'

❧ ✿ ✿ ✿ ✿ ✿ ❦

My host chain-smoked cigarettes as part of his breathing pattern, but he was not a jittery man; he exuded the contented aura of someone satisfied with their life's work. His clients came from all over the country, from Pathein in the west, Myitkyina in the north and Tarchilek in the east. If he was fully booked, they would stay overnight with relatives, or even sleep in their car and come back the next day. Min Wai read about twenty palms a day. He saw himself as an educator. 'I feel like I am performing a service to my community like a doctor or a teacher. I am here to educate people,' Min Wai told me. 'I make people see they have to make corrections in their life. I am proud of that.' Min Wai has always made himself popular with people who matter. He read the palms of local commanders who ensured he was not subjected to the same kind of intimidation and extortion that most people had to put up with. He advised entrepreneurs on the right time to start their businesses. If they found success, they would always remember how they got there. The white Toyota Corolla station wagon in front of his house, sheltered from the sun and rain by a sheet of corrugated iron, was a gift from a grateful client.

Min Wai traded in fatalism, an important part of the Burmese psyche. Did a belief in a predetermined life infantilise the Burmese people, keep their expectations low, hold them back from revolution? It certainly set them apart from Western thinking. The foreigners who came to see him didn't really believe in the concept of a past life, he said. 'What will happen in this life is already determined by what you have done in a previous life. This is what we Buddhists believe. For the Burmese the past life is really important. Foreigners only believe in the present life, they don't really understand the past life. For example, if a person digs up a ruby, that is because of what they did in a past life. But what they do with their ruby, that is up to them, that's their present life. You could pass it straight to the foreman and he would give you one lakh, but you could get five lakh at the ruby market, ten lakh in Rangoon, twenty lakh in Thailand, fifty lakh in Hong Kong and by the time it reached London it would be worth two hundred lakh. I can tell you if you are going to find the ruby, but I cannot tell you what to do with it. You have to make your own luck in the present life.'

When I visited Min Wai, Burma's new, nominally civilian government was in its infancy. It was six months after Burma's November 2010 elections, which, although flawed and unfair, had created a new administration led by former generals who had resigned their commission to run for office. The State Peace and Development Council had been officially dissolved. The despised junta leader Than Shwe had stepped down. The two-house *hlutthaw* had become the country's first functioning parliament since the 1962 coup, although its chambers were dominated by the military's proxy, the Union Solidarity and Development Party (USDP).

Across North Africa, the street revolutions of the Arab Spring were unseating long-entrenched autocratic leaders. What was unfolding in Burma, however, was a transformation from the top down, managed by the very people who had ruled with ineptitude and cruelty for so long. The Burmese people wanted to believe in change, but years of disappointment and countless false dawns had tempered their optimism. In his readings, Min Wai saw cause for hope. Diplomacy was useless, he said, these things were beyond the control of politicians. The Arab Spring was triggered by an auspicious planetary alignment, and when the right stars shone in Burmese skies, change would come. 'I have published my readings that something will happen,' he said. 'Right now is so-called democracy, but it is not real. The reign of the army will come to an end in 2015. True democracy will come then. If you talk about it at the UN, it will be useless. It's the stars and planets that dominate fate. Things change as the stars change. According to my calculation, there will be peace in 2015.'

I knew that I shouldn't really be giving credence to a four-dollar-a-session palm reader, however impressive his pedigree, but Min Wai's words were exciting. When I had arrived in Burma it was a country stripped of hope. An uprising had just been crushed; the despotic rulers seemed immovable. It would be another generation before the people could summon the courage and the energy to rise up again, political analysts had said. But in the hot season of 2011, although we hardly dared acknowledge it, we were starting to see signs of creeping change. March had seen the swearing-in of Burma's new president, Thein Sein, up to then known only as a pallid, bespectacled army general, content to follow orders, who had played his role in quelling the Saffron Uprising. But in a surprising inaugural address on 30 March, the now civilian President Thein Sein sketched out a vision of democratic rule and economic reform, and made conciliatory overtures to the opposition. The government proposed peace talks with armed rebels and had begun to free up restrictions on the press. In the new parliament building in Naypyidaw, a confection of tiered roofs and elaborate pillared pavilions, legislators stood up to demand improvements for their constituents – better roads, schools, hospitals.

A few months after he came to power, Thein Sein suspended the construction of the Myitsone Dam at the head of the Irrawaddy River. The dam was to generate electricity not for the energy-starved Burmese, but for the southern Chinese province of Yunnan, and the project had been deeply unpopular for its potentially adverse environmental impacts and the displacement of local people, all for the benefit of the Chinese economy. The suspension of the dam's construction, a rare concession to public pressure, was one of the first indicators of change. On the streets, people admitted to small improvements, a wary, intuitional sense of new freedom. But they had been disappointed before. These were small steps, and the people were still trying to work out whether the country's transition from military rule to what the state media described as 'discipline flourishing democracy' was real.

To have faith in the reforms, it seemed Burma's people needed a clearer understanding of their leaders' motivations for unwinding decades of authoritarian control. It was nearly four years since the uprising had been put down, and now the streets were quiet. There were few examples in history of military dictatorships voluntarily relinquishing power. Why was it happening now? The Burmese people and their rulers had lived in seclusion for half a century. For years, external pressure from other governments and the criticism of human rights groups seemed to have made little impact on the generals. But it was becoming increasingly difficult to ignore the desperate state of Burma's economy relative to its Asian neighbours – average income per head was less than $900 per year, and even lowly Laos had overtaken Burma in the development rankings. The Arab revolutions had unnerved the world's remaining autocrats, and General Than Shwe had confided to aides that he feared being marched off to an international tribunal. Squeezed by Western sanctions, the country's nationalistic leaders were developing a growing distaste for their heavy economic dependence on China. It appeared there was an earthly alignment that had persuaded the generals they had to change course. But Win Mai's explanation was written in celestial terms. 'People think that they change things by marching, voting, making speeches, but it comes from the stars,' he said. 'Only the stars.'

✿ ✿ ✿ ✿ ✿ ✿

Sitting with a cup of green tea, enjoying the scent of the frangipani flowers that had wound themselves around the wire mosquito grille, I hung around for a while, to watch Min Wai work. Soon he was drawn from his global prophesies to the more mundane grist of life. His front room office became busy with clients, none of whom seemed to require the privacy that others might seek when discussing their most personal affairs. A couple, who looked to be in their thirties, sat at Min Wai's desk for their consultation, their palms upturned. 'How many children will I have?' the wife asked.

'There will be four children,' Min Wai replied. 'First two daughters and later two sons.'

The woman concurred that she already had two daughters, but as her husband had been sterilised, she did not anticipate the sons. Min Wai's customary tact seemed to desert him; he was insistent, certain that two sons would follow.

The husband grew angry. 'Well you may have your two sons,' he told his wife. 'But those sons won't be mine!'

The couple began to fight, and the family waiting behind them looked down at their feet, sucking in their cheeks, stifling their giggles.

# 11
# Girl Power
# and the Revolution

The Me N Ma girls are running late. We are cutting across the north of town in a cab. I am scrunched up on one side, my left hip jammed up against the car door. Squashed to my right is a lavishly scented tangle of smooth long limbs and glossy black tresses of hair – three members of the band. Manicured nails flip open compacts; the girls scrutinise, retouch and preen and scold the driver for choosing the wrong route. They worry about me. 'Are you sure you're okay there, do you have enough room? Window up or down?' they purr. 'Would you like a cookie?'

Actually they're not really cookies, they are paper-thin bits of wafer. From the front passenger seat, Ah Moon, her inky black eyes accentuated by long, curled, mascaraed lashes, has twisted round to hand out the snacks. She pushes a piece towards Htike Htike, who shrieks as if a poisonous snake has been shoved in her face. 'That's too big!' she cries, and snaps off a corner. The two girls launch instantly into a shouting match in Burmese, but their playful expressions don't match the indignation of their noisy exchange.

'Are you okay?' I ask Htike Htike, who is squeezed next to me.

'Yes, fine!' she laughs and points a finger accusingly at Ah Moon. 'That girl is trying to make me fat.'

Boisterous and relaxed, and chair-dancing to R&B played on Htike Htike's phone, the girls are on their way to a lunch meeting set up by their Los Angeles manager. Shades of green rush past the window as the taxi nips along the short cut running through Rangoon University's decaying, overgrown campus. It all seems so normal. But when I ask them whether three years ago, when they first met, they could have pictured such a scene, they laugh, then quieten, and munch their wafers.

✤ ✿ ✿ ✿ ✿ ✤

There were signs from the start that the Australian dance teacher and the Burmese impresario didn't share quite the same vision for Burma's first girl band. Nikki May – blond, sun-kissed, exuberant – had landed in Rangoon almost at random. She was in her late twenties, backpacking around South-east Asia, and looking for somewhere further off the beaten track. She was on an adventure, keen to do some volunteering, to explore; she didn't have anything in particular mapped out. She found an apartment to share, hooked up to the Rangoon party scene, and began working in city orphanages, teaching dance and music to love-starved children in her easy, open, Melbournite style.

Moe Kyaw was a Burmese music producer, a marketing mogul of the Rangoon pop scene, who had had some success promoting rock bands and pop singers in the country's small but loyal popular music market. He had been following the rise of manufactured girl bands in South Korea and Singapore, groups modelled on the Spice Girls who sang upbeat dance numbers or harmonised ballads. Could the same thing work here? It was only when he got chatting to Nikki at a party that the idea really took shape. She had the artistic vision; he had the industry contacts. They knew it wouldn't be easy, and in Burma's conservative society there was a risk that it just wouldn't work at all. But they booked an audition space, advertised for young, talented singers and dancers, and waited.

On a clear Rangoon winter's morning in January 2010, 173 hopeful young women turned up to a bar named 50th Street, where the chairs were up on tables and cleaning ladies mopped away at the sticky, beery floor. There was to be an audition, X Factor-style, in front of Nikki and Moe Kyaw. 'Some were like models, just beautiful girls,' Htike Htike recalled. 'Some were shy, some were overconfident, some were just crazy.' Many of the girls were easy to dismiss, with their painful flat notes and rhythmless dancing. But when it came to the girls who showed promise, the judges didn't quite see eye to eye. Moe Kyaw was taken with the prettiest, most doll-like creatures, the ones with the palest skin, a trait demanded by the Asian perception of beauty; Nikki was looking for sass, energy and raw talent. In the end it was she who won the day. The demure girls went home disappointed, and five bright, feisty young women – Htike Htike, Ah Moon, Win Hnin, Cha Cha and Kimmy – were selected. A new band named the Tiger Girls was born.

✽ ✿ ✿ ✿ ✿ ✿ ✽

They came from different parts of the country, each born just after the failed uprising of 1988. All were from humble beginnings, but all were blessed with attentive, ambitious parents, determined that their children should succeed in education. Their childhoods were strict and austere. Win Hnin lived in a tiny, wooden-framed house with bamboo walls. Ah Moon grew up in a thin-aired village in the Himalayan foothills. Htike Htike shared a small Rangoon apartment with three generations of her family. In 1990s Burma there was no notion of 'pop stars' and no glamorous role models to aspire to. In Britain, the Spice Girls, the inventors of 'girl power' and the prototype for the global explosion of girl bands, were rising up the charts. But the five young Burmese girls, whose lives revolved around home and school, were unaware even of its existence. Kimmy, the most gifted singer in the group, grew up in the rural depths of Chin state, where her father and uncles hunted wild boar and peacocks. Sunday school was the social highlight of her week. Kimmy didn't hear a single pop song until she went to university. 'In my village we made our own music. My family are Christians and my father was the conductor of the church choir. I loved the choir. We always sang gospel songs and until I was about seventeen those were the only songs I had heard.' The girls studied hard at their painfully underfunded government schools and they all made it to university, gaining degrees in modern languages, zoology, computer science, chemistry and mathematics.

'All of our families value education above everything else,' said Htike Htike, a husky-voiced, plain-speaking twenty-five-year-old. 'I could have gone on to do a master's degree, but I stopped in order to become an artist. My family doesn't see singing as a safe career. Becoming a star doesn't exist in Burma. My parents have just about accepted what I do but there is still pressure. My aunty is always talking about it. She thinks a master's degree is more important than anything.' Ah Moon speaks Russian, English, French, Japanese, Burmese and her native Kachin. Her parents would have been intensely proud if she had landed a job at a foreign embassy in Rangoon, but instead, just as she began her job hunt, she heard about the girl band audition. 'I think I had always wanted to be a singer. When I was young I used to write and perform my own songs. I would sing as if I was onstage to anyone who would listen. But I never thought that could be my career, I didn't know there was a job like this.'

The Tiger Girls had a standard look: hotpants or short skirts, flimsy tops, sparkly heels. They were comfortable in their revealing clothes, confident in their graceful, lithe bodies. They were less comfortable about Moe Kyaw's insistence that their outfits matched. Their first songs were so-called 'copy tracks' – well-known Western pop tunes overlaid with sentimental Burmese lyrics. They found a cheap rehearsal space and Nikki choreographed their high-energy, synchronised dance routines. Their first gig was in Mandalay in the hot season of 2010, at an open-air festival to celebrate *Thingyan*, Burmese New Year. It was a big shock to the audience. 'When we were walking to the stage, someone shouted "Where are you from?" They thought we must be from another country, we didn't look like Burmese girls,' Win Hnin said. 'I shouted: "We are from Burma!"' It didn't go down well. The crowd threw plastic water bottles and slippers. There was a concern that the Tiger Girls were bringing foreign style to a country that had become insular and nativistic under military rule. 'This is a very traditional place,' Ah Moon said. 'The authorities tried to ban us, they didn't want us to appear in the newspapers.' The censorship board vetted their outfits and famously banned them from wearing coloured wigs. The disapproval came from the top, and it trickled right down through society. 'My daddy is a pastor,' Ah Moon said. 'In my village they are always asking him: "Why is your daughter doing this?"'

– ✿ ✿ ✿ ✿ ✿ –

The girls don't elaborate, but things quickly turned sour with their co-producer Moe Kyaw. There had been tensions from the start, over song choices, image and direction. The girls wanted to write their own material; Moe Kyaw, keen for quick commercial success, insisted on a stock repertoire of covers. But the main problem seemed to be that he still didn't think they were good-looking enough, and was frustrated when they failed to secure a deal to appear in a Burmese television commercial. It wasn't the band he had envisaged. None of the girls is classically beautiful – Kimmy is plump-faced and Htike Htike has a strong jaw – but they all exude a confidence and sexiness rare among Burmese women. With her liquid eyes and bee-stung lips, Ah Moon has a mesmerising look, which can switch from smiley to smouldering in the click of a camera lens. In 2011, Moe Kyaw and the girls split. The girls won't tell me the details, but Moe Kyaw, still nursing his dream of creating the perfect band, threatened to sue them over ownership of the Tiger Girls brand. Their mentor Nikki was still with them, but this was new territory, and a precarious time. Money was a problem, and the band members all tried to find other work to make cash for costumes and studio time. Kimmy crooned easy listening melodies in the lobbies of big Rangoon hotels; Htike Htike worked as a graphic designer. Most pressingly, the girls needed to find a new name for themselves. They all felt they wanted something that tied them to their country, and with Nikki's help came up with the Me N Ma Girls, a play on the country's official name.

It was a serendipitous choice. The rebranded group was launched just as Thein Sein's new civilian-fronted government began its ambitious reform programme, tugging the country away from the restrictions of the past. Delighted and somewhat baffled citizens saw the first shoots of civic freedoms: the release of some dissidents, the relaxation of censorship and an improvement in workers' rights. Burma was at last a place of possibility, and the patriotism embodied by the Me N Ma Girls hit just the right note. The girls felt they were representing a youthful, optimistic side of their country that the world had yet to see. 'The timing was perfect. Just before things started changing we chose our name. It's obvious what it means. And with everything that has happened, we're now even prouder of our country,' Htike Htike said.

≈ ✿ ✿ ✿ ✿ ✿ ≈

Free from Moe Kyaw's diktats, the girls started to experiment with their own songwriting. With inspiration from the music of Beyoncé, Bruno Mars, Taylor Swift and the Pussycat Dolls, they created an easy, electro-pop sound, with R&B influences and harmonised melodies. But it was their lyrics that marked them out. 'We don't just want to sing about broken hearts,' said Cha Cha. 'Now we are quite political. We want to show what is happening to our people, to our country.' One of the first songs they wrote together was a ballad, 'Come Back Home'. The gentle, poignant song addressed Burmese exiles – the doctors, engineers and businessmen, who, seeing no future for their families in Burma's drowning economy, had escaped over the decades to new lives in the United States, Australia or Singapore. But as the new Burma set out on the path of political reform and economic recovery, it needed all the help it could get, the Me N Ma Girls reasoned. 'There are so many brains out there, so many talented people who are Burmese. We're asking all the clever people to come back, to help rebuild our country now that conditions are changing. There are still problems, it may not be easy, but we are saying it is time,' Ah Moon told me. Amateur footage of a touching performance of 'Come Back Home' is on YouTube, filmed at a lunch hosted by the US ambassador in Rangoon. The girls had been invited to an upmarket Italian restaurant in a colonial house set amid coconut palms on the north side of Inya Lake. They dressed appropriately for the occasion, in formal Burmese fitted blouses and ankle-length silk sarongs, their glossy hair neatly styled. After the lunch, tables were pushed aside to make room for their impromptu performance. Kimmy was seated on a restaurant chair playing the acoustic guitar and the other girls were gathered around her, singing harmonies. The diplomats dabbed their eyes. 'We never had the chance to write about politics before,' Ah Moon said. 'But now we can and we're excited to do that. When we sang the song for the embassy people, some of them were crying. There's a lot of hope in this country now, and I think they could feel that.'

✿ ✿ ✿ ✿ ✿ ✿

On a concrete landing, a glittery pile of platform sandals and kitten heels heaped outside the door marked the apartment. Inside was a typical Rangoon flat with heavily varnished, teakwood furniture arranged around the edge of the room and a crocheted white cloth draped over the huge wide screen TV. A framed, embroidered message, 'Prayer Changes Things', hung above a glass-fronted cabinet. The apartment was rented by Ah Moon's father – the pastor – who had moved to the city to preach in an evangelical church. The Me N Ma Girls were sprawled on wooden benches with their long legs curled up beneath them. Before I met them, I had conjured up an image of the girls as ditzy and spoiled, but my preconception was quickly dispelled. These girls were charming, funny and sweetly supportive of one another. When one talked, the others listened carefully, boosting each other with affirming nods, rounds of high fives and frequent bouts of giggles.

Things were going well for the girls. Representing, as they did, a new, freer Burma, they had enjoyed a burst of international publicity, spawning a mini South-east Asian tour. Defying convention that forbids women from travelling without a chaperone, they flew unaccompanied to their first destination – Bangkok. They marvelled at the high rises, the sky train and embraced the sense of freedom, but found some of the city's excesses just too much. 'Bangkok was wild, it felt free,' said Htike Htike. 'It was great to wear just what we wanted, but some of the things there were shocking – even to us.' Cha Cha suffered the most severe case of culture shock. The zoology major, an expert in marine life and traditional Burmese dancing, was dizzied by Bangkok's brash sensory overload. On an ill-advised outing to Nana Plaza, a concrete complex packed with seedy, neon-lit go-go bars, she witnessed a live sex act that sent her running to the Ladies to throw up.

Their next stop was Singapore, where the ordered cityscape, pixellated billboards and conspicuous consumption provided more evidence of Burma's backwardness. The pavements were smooth and swept, traffic islands immaculately planted with shrubs and flowers, waste bins colour coded. Everything looked brand new, and everybody looked clean, styled and wealthy. The unfortunate contrast to Rangoon was a little disconcerting for the girls, who still clung on to their patriotic message and the hope that things would get better at home. 'Seeing these other places has opened our eyes, it has made us think about what life is like in Burma,' said Win Hnin. 'But then it makes us stronger. I see good in what we are doing. We want our country to be known around the world. We want to show that it has something; that it's not just backward and poor.'

The Me N Ma girls performed at a Singapore football stadium ahead of a match between Burmese national league club KBZ and a team from the Philippines. At a safe distance from disapproving eyes, they wore their most revealing stage outfits to date, very short skirts and midriff tops. 'My parents weren't there and I won't show them the pictures!' Cha Cha said. But the girls – most of them – enjoyed the look. 'We bought some new outfits and we were all okay apart from Kimmy, she kept trying to pull her skirt, to make it longer.' The girls laughed, including Kimmy, who fiddled with one of the three crosses around her neck. 'I was not okay,' she confirmed.

They returned home to find their photograph on the front cover of a Burmese current affairs magazine (thankfully not wearing their Singapore outfits). To be taken so seriously, for their existence to be regarded as having political value, was a thrill. In those exciting months it seemed as if they were breaching milestone after milestone, each time surpassing their expectations of what a Burmese pop band could be. Foreign journalists, now at liberty to report from Burma, buzzed around them. The band was the perfect, photogenic emblem of the new government's paper reforms. Eight thousand miles away in Los Angeles, music producer Daniel Hubbert, CEO of Surfbreak Entertainment, was sitting in the Californian sunshine with his morning coffee and a copy of the *LA Times*. He read about the girls and was intrigued.

❧ ✿ ✿ ✿ ✿ ✿ ❦

By early 2013 the Me N Ma Girls were in Los Angeles, wearing their new power sunglasses and trailing on foot around Beverly Hills with faces upturned to the sky. 'We were staring at the trees,' said Ah Moon. 'Not the houses, we couldn't believe the big, beautiful, perfect trees, all in a row, all the same.' Hubbert had signed the girls to Power Music Inc., and the band had travelled to Los Angeles to record three new songs, including their new anthem 'Girl Strong'. Hubbert, who described the girls as 'raw, the real deal', also wanted to professionalise them a little. He had suggestions about image, expressed horror at their carbohydrate-laden, rice-stoked diet, and introduced them to yoga. Htike Htike's slightly rounded butt and muscular thighs, envied in Burma as the perfect mould for a snug-fitting sarong, had to be slimmed down, Daniel had told her. 'Her thighs are bigger than what he needs,' Ah Moon said bluntly, making everyone laugh, including the slender Htike Htike. From LA they flew to New York, to play at a women's empowerment event at the Lincoln Center, a blur of excitement they recount carefully, methodically as if it had been a dream.

❧ ✿ ✿ ✿ ✿ ✿ ❦

With their international record deals and increasing influence, what is next for the girls? Can a political revolution be followed by a social, sexual revolution in conservative Burma, and are the girls ready to lead it? Their song 'Sense of Shit', a clumsy play on the word censorship, accuses Burmese people of not only tolerating years of government censorship but censoring their own behaviour. 'It's about marrying the guy your parents want you to marry, not speaking out, bowing your head,' said Ah Moon. But the girls are surprisingly reticent about pushing the boundaries of acceptability. They don't regard themselves as social revolutionaries and a permissive, Western society is not for Burma, they are firm about that. They even fret about the decline in moral standards that laxer restrictions could bring. 'Now you can see some really bad horror movies and sexy movies. They are not suitable to show in Burma,' said Kimmy, primly. The others concur. 'Lip kissing is not suitable to show in our culture. This is very shameful for us. We understand this can happen in an American movie but not here. We want to keep our tradition. We don't want to watch Burmese girls dancing in their bikinis and we are never going to dress like that. We have to be true to ourselves.'

The girls will never wear bikinis in public, they will never be photographed tripping drunkenly out of nightclubs in the early hours of the morning, and there will certainly never be any sex tapes. But they are still challenging convention in Burma. Their celebrity aura, their boisterous manner, their tottering-heeled glamour are all new in a country where many still believe that girls who dance in public are prostitutes. Do they have boyfriends? They are reluctant to say. Ah Moon attempts to explain how things work. 'We can't have boyfriends,' she begins. 'But actually all of us do, except for Kimmy.' They roll with laughter at Ah Moon's contradictory statement, wiping tears from the corners of their eyes with manicured fingertips. 'Boyfriends are difficult. They are not really allowed in our society,' Htike Htike explains. The others nod. 'If you decide to marry him, then you can introduce him to your family and neighbours. But at the moment, there's no way I can introduce my boyfriend to them. He doesn't exist. My boyfriend is an army doctor. I've known him since childhood. We can meet in the teashop, we might go and eat noodles together. Anything else is not allowed. It's like we are living two different lives.'

Htike Htike's family lives in a small apartment in a middle-income district of Rangoon. It's not bad, it has running water, an intermittent electricity supply and stays dry in the monsoon. Framed graduation photos of Htike Htike and her elder brother are proudly displayed in the main living room with a flowered, lino floor. An old television and

VCR are the centrepiece of the room, a few chairs are pushed up against the wall but the family prefer to sit on the ground, cooled by an upright, rotating fan. Beyond the living room is a narrow corridor, leading to three sleeping compartments, partitioned by plywood walls that do not reach the ceiling. There is little privacy. Htike Htike lives with her parents and grandparents. 'I come from a strict family,' she says. 'I can't wear short skirts at home, no way. At home I always wear a *longyi* over the top.' Htike Htike is often out late with her boyfriend or her band mates, a constant source of tension. 'I have hidden an extra set of keys outside. I usually wait until my grandfather is asleep and sneak in then. My parents always scold me, but they are very caring. They will call me this lunchtime and ask me if I have eaten. If I don't reply they will text me, and I know they won't start their lunch until I reply.'

# 12
# We Are Not Afraid

I climb the narrow concrete staircase to the door of Zayar's office on the corner of 49th Street. My former fixer is there to meet me. He seems taller. He is definitely more confident, expansive. His voice is louder. He's smiling more. It is the rainy season; the sky is grey, but the air is fresh, cleansed by the daily downpours. A red flame tree is in bloom outside the open balcony window. We are one floor up, just far enough above the street for the cries of hawkers and the hubbub of the pavement teashop to be more of a comforting soundtrack than an intrusion. This is the office of *Maw Kun* (the *Chronicle*), Burma's first new political magazine for sixty years. Red-spined copies of *Maw Kun's* first issues are stacked on a table, pleasingly thick and professional-looking with striking cover designs. 'Someone said it's the Burmese *New Yorker*,' Zayar says, laughing and colouring with pride.

Zayar, just a few years ago a junior reporter, is now the editor of *Maw Kun*, and the boss of the half-dozen journalists sitting at their laptops along a row of trestle tables. It is a modest, neat office. Zayar has already whisked my wet umbrella from my hand to put in its special stand; shoes are tidily stacked on a rack by the door. The printed A4 papers spread out across Zayar's desk are scrawled with red ink, words encircled, others crossed out, notes scribbled in the margins – he is proofreading the next issue. Maps of Rangoon, Mandalay, Naypyidaw, Burma and the World are taped to the green tiled walls. The fluorescent strip lights are on, while the upright fans stand idle. It is one of the blessed few weeks of the year in Rangoon when there is no need for buzzing fans and air conditioning.

✦ ✿ ✿ ✿ ✿ ✿ ✦

The previous year had brought a transformation of Burma's media landscape – one of the clearest manifestations of the government's reform programme. Taking their cue from President Thein Sein's surprisingly radical speeches on the need for change, bureaucrats in the ministries across Naypyidaw were struck by the realisation that the status quo was simply not sustainable. Nowhere was this message clearer than in the Ministry of Information, the crucible of censorship in Burma, which had long sought to shape the mindset of the Burmese populace by controlling their access to news, opinion and knowledge. In recent years, their efforts had been subverted by technology – mobile phones, satellite television and, most decisively, the Internet – which, although available only to a few, had already made a dramatic impact on Burmese society. Following the failed uprising of 2007 and the catastrophe of Cyclone Nargis in 2008, a lively cyber community of bloggers and Facebookers had emerged. While avoiding the blatant political references that could land them in jail, they carefully documented the unpalatable truths of their lives and the frustrations of blackouts, unemployment, a neglected education system and poverty. On their side was the regime's haphazard approach to controlling the Internet and their own superior technical knowledge. This fast-moving world of digital publishing had raced far from the grasp of the censor. The Ministry of Information, home to the hated Press Scrutiny Board, bowed to the inevitable. Within months of the new government taking power in 2011, ministry officials began to draw up a timetable for the abolition of censorship.

For Zayar, it was impeccable timing. For several years he had nurtured a dream of starting a political magazine. Until 2011 the dream was pure fantasy, but suddenly he saw that he could actually make it happen. With his colleague Nyan Lin he started to put together a small, enthusiastic team of reporters who wanted to move beyond the reactive, shallow news stories that were the grist of the Burmese press. 'We felt that the stories we were writing were like an iceberg,' Zayar said. 'The big stuff was under the water. There was breaking news but no one ever thought harder than that, there was no analysis, no in-depth investigations.' Zayar secured a small grant from an international organisation keen to promote open media in Burma, put down a deposit on office space, advertised for junior reporters and applied to the Ministry of Information for a publishing licence. Burma's first new political magazine since 1952 was conceived.

❧ ✿ ✿ ✿ ✿ ✿ ☙

On 24 August 2012, just four days after half a century of press censorship was lifted, Zayar walked in the rain to the small Indian-run printing shop on 19th street to pick up the first issue of *Maw Kun*. The copy was still warm in his hands as he flipped through the pages, pursing his lips to suppress a smile. Over the years, Burmese magazine editors had tried to circumvent editorial restrictions by focusing on literature and entertainment. Writers had become adept at producing fictional short stories with oblique political messages – and they had to be very oblique because any hint of dissent could have landed both writer and editor in jail. But with its direct reporting of political issues, *Maw Kun* was something completely fresh. The aim was to explain the key issues of the day to the Burmese people, and to influence the decision makers in government who were steering the country's transformation. Zayar sent complimentary copies of the magazine to twenty-seven ministries in Naypyidaw, and to the president's office. He made sure the magazine was distributed across Burma's remote provinces, from the Himalayan foothills of Kachin state to the breezy fishing villages of the Tenasserim. He wanted the reach of this physical, printed magazine to be as wide as possible – while there had been an explosion of information and political comment online in Burma, only around 1 per cent of the population was connected to the Internet.

The magazine's crusading, challenging tone was revolutionary. One of the first issues questioned why, with Burma being a diverse, multi-religious society, a daily prayer to Lord Buddha was compulsory in state schools. A front-page story examined the future of Arakan, or Rakhine state, which had been torn apart by ethnic violence. Zayar spent two months researching a story about Burma's thousands of street children, whose existence had been ignored by the state-controlled press. His reporters carried out an investigation into the safety of the country's food and the unregulated use of pesticides and fertiliser. With each story, he was breaking new ground. 'We dig deeper and deeper to investigate issues that are important to the people. We want to get new angles from behind the scenes and reach decision-makers with our findings,' Zayar said. *Maw Kun* also made some pioneering style innovations, such as introducing the first photo essays to the Burmese press, while Zayar encouraged his reporters to use direct quotes – a standard reporting technique for journalists anywhere else, but unheard of in Burma. 'Before we would not dare quote what officials actually said from their mouths, that was like looking at them straight in the eyes, it was too bold,' Zayar said. Instead the journalists would faithfully reproduce the government's propaganda statements, or copy out the generals' long speeches verbatim, not daring to edit out a thing.

There were soon signs that *Maw Kun* was attracting an enthusiastic readership. The education minister phoned up and asked for a copy, universities and embassies sought subscriptions, and would-be readers knocked on the door of the magazine's office to buy issues after they had sold out on the newsstand. Zayar's influence was growing. In the old days, when he needed a response from officials to a story he was writing, he would go through the hollow exercise of putting his questions into a letter. He would rarely get a response. Now he could call up ministries directly and get an instant comment. Every ministry had a spokesman, a spin doctor. While many in government may have harboured distaste for this budding era of openness, it was clear the media's power was on the rise.

⊱ ✿ ✿ ✿ ✿ ✿ ⊰

Zayar may seem like a radical, but he comes from a line of government workers, and would still be one himself, had his wife got her way. His family has for generations been tied to Rangoon's port, which in the early twentieth century had once been one of the world's most vibrant hubs, handling exports of rice and timber and imports of European luxuries for colonial civil servants. His grandfather was the Port Authority's doctor, his father was in the engineering department, his mother in the commercial department. His wife Aye Aye is an accountant and works in the Port Authority's colonial headquarters, an imposing neo-classical building on the riverfront. Her office, with its twelve-foot-high wooden-shuttered windows flung open to receive the salty breeze, is stacked with piles of papers, some three or four feet high, without a single computer in sight.

Aided by the nepotism that was one of the few perks of a government position, Zayar secured his first job at the Port Authority at the age of eighteen. His first task was clearing up the shipyard. In Rangoon's unforgiving heat this was tough, back-breaking work and came with a pitiful starting salary of 600 kyat per month – in those days equivalent to just a few dollars. But Zayar rose quickly through the ranks. By the age of twenty-five, he was working in the marine department, regulating the passage of ocean liners in and out of the port, the youngest employee ever to hold such a position. His official salary was 38,000 kyat, with the opportunity to make it up to 150,000 (only around $150, but far above an average salary) by soliciting tea money. 'This was standard. The ship operators expected to give them, we expected to receive them. This was just the way the system worked,' Zayar said. The same year, in 2005, he married Aye Aye, the quiet, serious girl from accounts. 'It was just after we got married that I talked to my wife. I told her, "This is not my dream. I want to be a journalist. Can you be patient with me for a few years?"'

Aye Aye was shocked. She had expected her marriage to bring her security. Their government positions were effectively jobs for life, and while their salaries were no more than comfortable, they had a guaranteed income and had been allocated a small but well-positioned room just five minutes' walk from the office. In her mind, her future was mapped out: she hoped to start a family, perhaps save a little and move somewhere a bit bigger. She protested, but Zayar was insistent, and eventually she acquiesced. With no journalistic experience, he was lucky to find his first job, as a reporter for the privately owned newspaper *Modern Weekly*. Zayar's starting salary was 30,000 kyat, around thirty dollars, with no possibility of making any extra. He was the happiest he had ever been.

✿ ✿ ✿ ✿ ✿ ✿ ✿

Zayar's successful establishment of *Maw Kun* was just one example of the many ways in which it was becoming clear that Aung San Suu Kyi's release had ushered in a new era. In August 2011, Thein Sein had initiated a dialogue with the freed opposition leader, paving the way, six months later, for her to fight and win an historic by-election in which she emphatically beat a Union Solidarity and Development Party candidate in the constituency of Kawhmu, south of Rangoon. In all, Suu Kyi's National League for Democracy won forty-three out of forty-five contested seats, proving the party's popularity to be as strong as ever in its first electoral test since the 1990 victory that the generals ignored. The following month, the former prisoner Suu Kyi took her seat in the lower house of the Naypyidaw parliament alongside nearly four dozen other new MPs from her party.

It was a frustrating time to be leaving Rangoon. My husband's contract was coming to an end and our family was heading back to London. The city that had been our home for more than three years was revelling in a new era of openness. In a nation of instinctive conversationalists, it was as if a volume switch had been steadily turned up on Burmese chatter, from mute to whispers to guarded exchanges around tea tables to debates, ever louder and more heated. Hands once clasped in rigid fear were released into the air to emphasise important points; eyes could focus directly on the fellow interlocutor rather than dart left and right to check for eavesdroppers. It was no longer likely that you would be denounced and imprisoned for saying the wrong thing. The government had authorised a bill approving peaceful demonstrations, and in Rangoon and Mandalay, demonstrators took to the streets, unafraid, in candlelit marches to protest against chronic power cuts. For most people, freedom from fear – a phrase coined long ago by Aung San Suu Kyi – was the first tangible dividend of Burma's political transition. 'We are not afraid,' Zayar told me. 'We are free to talk in the teashops, in the street, on the phone. Whatever we want, wherever we want.'

This was the first time that Zayar had told me about his work for the 'exile media' – the opposition news organisations that beamed back their uncensored news into Burma through all the years of dictatorship. Zayar had simply wanted to tell Burma's story. At home, he was thwarted by censorship. The government had no wish to see a true reflection of its dysfunctional society in the media. So journalists like Zayar had to look beyond Burma's borders for outlets for their work. He had reported for the Democratic Voice of Burma, and the Delhi-based Burmese website Mizzima. But even these organisations exerted a form of editorial control that Zayar found restricting. 'What they wanted was not always an accurate picture of our life, of our society. Those organisations were run by activists, and every story had to have an anti-government message. Some of their stories were not balanced.'

❧ ✿ ✿ ✿ ✿ ✿ ❧

As editor of his own magazine, free from censorship or editorial interference, Zayar now has independence, a thrilling and unexpected position to be in. 'We don't set out to make a point, we set out to look for the truth,' he says. When he talks about *Maw Kun*, his words tumble out, he's excited and jumps around topics. His chatter is peppered with nervous laughter – wonder that all this is happening. These days, Zayar can hardly keep up with his own thoughts. The magazine is breaking ground by investigating issues the Burmese press had never dared touch before. By the fourth issue, *Maw Kun* had already run articles about land grabs, sectarian violence, corruption and human trafficking. These would be bread-and-butter stories in similar publications in other developing countries, but in Burma it was new territory. 'These are subjects we always knew existed, but we couldn't write about them. We would just lose time, energy and money. We couldn't touch them in the past.' *Maw Kun* has even won its first award, and Zayar proudly shows me a framed certificate for 'Excellence in Journalism' from Burma's brave, embattled Gay and Lesbian Association, in gratitude for an article Zayar wrote about their struggles. 'I carried out an investigation into what it's like to be gay in Burma – the prejudices, the stigma, the problems. Of course there is a big gay community here, but until now it wasn't acknowledged,' Zayar said. 'I tried to write this story four or five years ago, but my editors told me, "Don't waste your time."'

✿ ✿ ✿ ✿ ✿ ✿

Zayar was not just writing about the changes in Burma, he was living them. As a journalist, he no longer had to skulk in the shadows. Zayar had always written under a pen name, Saw Thit Htoo, an ethnic Karen name that could be roughly translated as 'Special New Scoop'. Of course, it would have been easy for the authorities to discover his real identity if they had wanted to; it was just better not to invite trouble. There were so many ways in which the authorities could make life difficult for individuals. For example, under the junta's rules, every household in Burma had been required to complete a Form 10, a document listing each permanent resident. The Form 10 would be registered with the local office of the State Peace and Development Council. Those listed on the form were the only ones allowed to sleep in the house – any visitors had to seek permission to stay overnight, and if permission was denied they had to leave the house by nine o'clock in the evening and return to the home where they were registered.

The system sat uncomfortably with Burma's easy-going traditions of hospitality, in which a convivial evening with friends could end without fuss with the unfurling of an extra bamboo sleeping mat for a spontaneous overnight stay. But the rules were strictly enforced. Armed police would carry out unannounced checks of apartments and houses to ensure the sleeping inhabitants matched the household list. These night-time raids, referred to by the population simply as 'Form 10s', had a menacing effect. There would be a loud bang on the door. Children curled up inside mosquito nets, grandfathers snoring under electric fans would be suddenly awakened, confused, the white beams of police torches blinding their sleepy eyes. There would be demands, questions, and, even if everything were in order, it would still be a disquieting experience. A Burmese friend of mine, out of sorts one day, explained her red eyes and uncharacteristic lethargy with a tight smile: 'Sorry – we got a Form 10 last night.' Of course, the system was a powerful form of control. In theory, the authorities knew the whereabouts of everyone, every night. Those most frequently targeted for 'guest checks' were potential subversives: opposition activists, journalists, musicians, artists and community workers. At times of heightened security concerns and paranoia among the junta, the frequency of raids would increase. As a journalist, Zayar would have been subject to particular scrutiny. 'My occupation on my Form 10 has always said trader,' he said. 'I would never write reporter, it was just too dangerous.'

Times had changed. The following Monday, Zayar's daughter Tone Tone Chit, born amidst the turmoil of Cyclone Nargis, would begin her education at Botataung Township Basic Education School No 1. Her new shoes, a regulation white blouse and knee-length green skirt were laid out ready in the family's small home. Her mother had tamed the five-year-old's fine black hair with a sensible pudding-bowl cut. When Zayar went to the school to enrol his daughter, he was handed a set of forms. He sat down at a low school desk in a classroom, empty for the summer holidays. The questions were straightforward enough, until he reached 'Occupation of Father'. He paused. He looked out of the window, through the rusting mosquito netting, to where the sun fell on the small concrete yard where his daughter would play. For the first time on an official form he dared to reveal he was a journalist. 'I wrote "Editor, *Maw Kun*." I felt proud and sick at the same time.'

❧ ✿ ✿ ✿ ✿ ✿ ❧

While marvelling at these small, positive steps, Zayar was phlegmatic about the practical impact of Burma's political transition on his family. He was now a father of two: his baby son was eight months old. His family was still crammed in a ten-by-fifteen-foot room. His priorities, his worries were just like anyone else's. Uppermost was the education system, so dreadfully undermined and neglected under military rule that it had already spawned what was mournfully referred to as a 'lost generation'.

Burma's generals had set the tone for their relationship with academia shortly after they seized power in 1962. On the morning of 8 July, they sent soldiers to dynamite the Student Union building of Rangoon University, retribution for a peaceful demonstration the day before by students concerned about falling standards. The regime's attacks on education continued apace for the next half-century. Schools and universities were desperately underfunded: government spending on education accounted for a tiny fraction of the annual budget, while at least 30 per cent was earmarked for military spending. Universities, feared by the junta as breeding grounds for subversion, were intermittently closed down and standards systematically eroded. On a visit to Mandalay University's main library, an academic friend of mine watched as the sole librarian locked away the small collection of books in a cupboard at closing time. Across the country, schools were left to decay. Teachers' salaries were so low (averaging around fifteen dollars a month) that a student's grades were often more a reflection of their parents' ability to stump up money for bribes than of their academic ability.

With her family unable to afford a private school – the choice today of any middle-class Burmese family who can scrape together the $1,000 annual fees charged by the most budget establishments – Tone Tone Chit was about to start her education in a government school much like the one her father had attended. The classroom would be bare, the teachers uninspiring and unhesitating in their willingness to use the cane or the slipper to enforce discipline. Even at the age of five, Tone Tone Chit would be required to sit perfectly still with her classmates at ancient wooden desks. Learning would be by rote. 'This is a parrot-learning state,' Zayar said. 'If you reproduce what the teacher says, even if you don't understand it, you will pass.'

The next edition of *Maw Kun* would tackle the issue of Burma's educational decline, possibly its greatest burden. Even in a country that values education above all else, it will take a generation for the poorly schooled populace to catch up with the rest of the world. The education budget has been doubled, but it is still lamentably inadequate and a tiny fraction of the government's spending on defence. There are computer science graduates whose professors were the only ones allowed to touch the PCs, doctors who have qualified without going near a patient. *Maw Kun* runs a regular section on 'Things We Have Forgotten', and, along with the red post-box and the school slate, there was a piece on university dorms, which all but disappeared after the military government restricted attendance at urban campuses in favour of so-called 'distance learning', in which the students were given audio cassettes to take home.

'We need a psychological change. This system has made us unquestioning, uncritical. We are followers. I personally, I was one of them. I had to force myself out. I had to do it alone. But as a nation, it's hard for us to break out,' Zayar says. 'In our next issue we want to come up with ideas, we are speaking to professors, teachers, students, education experts… We want to help. We want the decision-makers to hear us.' Zayar believes in a shared responsibility in the struggle to create a new, better Burma. 'We are all responsible for reform, not just the government, all the people. And it is our responsibility in the media to persuade the people that their own contribution is important.'

☙ ✿ ✿ ✿ ✿ ✿ ❧

The light starts to fade and a black cloud of crows swarms to the trees outside Zayar's office window. The birds settle on their perches and begin a chorus of noisy squawking, a daily ritual and prelude to the rapid, tropical nightfall. Zayar leans back in his white plastic chair. He is silent for a moment. His life has changed so much, he has so much to tell me, but he's searching for the perfect anecdote, so that I really understand.

U Tint Swe was a man loathed and feared by every Burmese journalist. Round-faced, with a school-boyish crown of hair, he was a faithful servant of the military government and head of the Press Scrutiny Board until its dissolution in 2012. His duty was clear, and, with a pot of sharpened pencils on his desk, he carried out his work with precision and dedication. 'This was the man who had power over my life,' Zayar grins. 'He was the one who cut my stories. He cut so many of my stories, I can't even count them.'

Zayar had rarely spoken directly to U Tint Swe, known for his bad temper and sharp tongue. The chief censor's bidding was carried out through his scores of underlings, most of them women, who trawled through every news article with their red pens in hand. But then, in late 2012, Zayar received a call on his mobile phone. It was U Tint Swe. 'At first I couldn't speak at all, I was so shocked that he was calling me,' Zayar said. 'He was very friendly. He asked about my magazine, he asked about my family.'

U Tint Swe said he was helping to organise a conference about the future of the media in Burma, and the purpose of the phone call was to invite Zayar to moderate one of the sessions with him.

'I did it,' Zayar said. 'I sat with U Tint Swe, like police and thief together. At the end, he thanked me, he shook my hand. That's when I thought: Now things have changed.'

# 13
# It's Not Easy Being a Punk

The first time I saw Darko he was on stage at Club 369, opposite the Chinese market. To be introduced first to his sweaty, shouty performance persona made the thoughtful, solicitous man I met later all the more intriguing. Darko's punk band, Side Effect, was playing support to a Montreal-based indie group, the Handsome Furs, who were in town for one night only. Burma, blighted by its pariah image, obscurity and disobliging bureaucracy, was not on the itinerary of any big international names, in fact, of any international names at all. To anyone's recollection, this was the first time a foreign band had played in Rangoon (a much anticipated visit from Engelbert Humperdinck failed to come off), and the evening attracted an eclectic crowd of foreign diplomats and aid workers plus the city's small, indigenous community of hardcore punks.

The gig was a leap into new territory, and a great success. The grimy club, its black walls sweating lager, could not have been the Handsome Furs' grandest venue, but the band seemed charmed by the unexpected, gentle hospitality they had received. Behind its iron-fisted reputation, they had discovered Burma's secret humanity. 'Thank you, from the bottom of our fucking hearts,' the female singer croaked at the end of their touchingly earnest, synth-based set. But it was Side Effect – bare-chested and tattooed – who stole the night. Their raw, guitar-fuelled sound (their music evokes Green Day or the Strokes) electrified the crowd, which surrendered to a rare sensation of freedom. In the heaving mosh pit, Britain's cultural attaché, well into middle age, pogoed joyfully with some of Rangoon's perfectly Mohicaned and pierced punks, who could have been teleported from the King's Road of the 1970s. For drummer Tser Htoo, it was a chance to use a full kit instead of his usual piles of books of differing heights. Darko, the frontman, leapt around the stage, leaning out in screaming communion with the front row and then skidding with his guitar on his knees to elicit some blaring feedback from the speaker. All around, the audience surprised themselves with their involuntary yells and bouts of headbanging. '*Chezuuube!*' 'Thank you!' Darko shouted. But the 369 did not rock till dawn. At 11 p.m. the lights came up on this island of anarchy – police regulations, we were told – and quickly we were back in the regulated Rangoon we knew, our heads pulsating with the glorious memory.

*✦ ✿ ✿ ✿ ✿ ✿ ✦*

There was an unfinished air to Darko's neighbourhood of high-rise apartments painted peach and pastel green. I waited outside his block, and right on time, he strolled up the street in black jeans and T-shirt, a pork-pie hat perched at a perfect angle on his head. Darko is skinny and handsome, with a beautiful white-toothed smile. He is an unfailingly courteous punk, with instinctive good manners. He greeted me and held open the door to a lobby that still smelt of paint and concrete dust. We took the lift to the fifth floor. This was a new, middle-class neighbourhood, but still a group of mangy dogs had gathered outside Darko's padlocked door. He shooed them off with a swing of his foot and they limped reluctantly away. He unlocked the door and directed me to a soft, grey velour-covered sofa. He disappeared off to the kitchen and returned with a glass of chilled water, which he placed carefully on a lace coaster on the coffee table in front of me.

Darko's singing career began by chance. He was a student at Rangoon's University of Foreign Languages, bored and uninspired by the daily routine of rote lectures in windowless, airless lecture halls. He was studying English, but the course gave no opportunity for him to speak the language, merely to listen to second-rate lecturers, hardly fluent themselves, drone on about the subjunctive. You could obtain a first-class degree there without uttering a single sentence. Sitting at home on his concrete floor, Darko started writing songs with his acoustic guitar. His friend heard them, and, fancying himself as a rock star, booked a studio for them to go and record some tracks. But it was Darko, not his friend, who emerged as the singer. 'It turned out he couldn't sing at all,' Darko smiled, leaning in to flick ash from a Red Ruby cigarette into a glass ashtray. 'In the studio he totally fucked up. He gave up, so I decided to sing them for myself. My songwriting is a bit strange anyway, so only I could really get the style right. Only I can really represent my songs.'

Probably thanks more to his forensic study of popular music than his degree, Darko speaks excellent, idiomatic English in a gravelly drawl. His first musical inspiration, he said, came from Kurt Cobain; his drive came from a desire to break out of the conformity of Burmese society. He was sick of listening to cover songs, the staple of the Burmese music scene – Western rock songs dubbed over with syrupy lyrics. 'That's all we had when I was growing up. I just didn't want to listen to that shit any more.'

Darko was raised in a Burmese timewarp. Ne Win's eccentric political blueprint took the once cosmopolitan country down a path of isolation and regression. In 1988, seven-year-old Darko watched from his window as a mass of student protesters, some with scarves wrapped around their faces, marched past his apartment building. He saw his neighbours prepare slingshots and bows and arrows and build bamboo barricades at the end of the street, ready to defend the community against government soldiers. His school was closed. When he heard the first bullets his mother shouted to him to hide under the bed with his baby brother. The uprising was crushed, ushering in a new military junta to be led by General Than Shwe, and with it a market-based economic system but an era of more rigorous political suppression. 'That brought the Dark Ages. That was what it was when I was growing up. There was no system then, just a dictatorship,' Darko said. Through the 1990s, Burma went further into retreat. As indie sounds such as Pulp and Garbage exploded around the globe, Darko was trapped in enforced seclusion. The only MTV he knew about was the unrelentingly dull Myanmar Television, and the Internet would not appear in Burma until well into the twenty-first century. 'We missed out on the 1990s rock thing. In the 1990s in Burma, we listened to '80s rock. That was when I was in high school. My favourite band was Guns n' Roses. Can you believe that?' he asked, recoiling at his own bad taste. 'We missed out.'

The teenaged Darko sensed there was more out there, and he sniffed out new music with the commitment of a bloodhound. On Saturday mornings, he would leave his schoolfriends and take a bus downtown to trawl through Rangoon's three small music stalls in Bogyoke Aung San Market, carrying with him a stack of blank cassette tapes. Browsing through the old LPs and precious cassettes, he came across the same people week after week, guys a few years older than him, cooler than him. They would sit on a litter-strewn embankment by the rail track behind the market, smoking cigarettes, swigging beer from brown glass bottles, listening to music on a small boom box. To save the battery, rewinding and forwarding would always be done by winding the tape round with a pencil. Darko had to put up with their condescending remarks, but he didn't care; he listened, he devoured their scraps of wisdom. If they recommended a new band, he would search for the music, hand over his tape, a few kyat, and then go back the following week to pick up the recording. But there was only so much he could do. Some bands just didn't reach Burma. While rock fans on other continents were discovering Korn and Limp Bizkit, Darko had to make do with Meatloaf and Bryan Adams.

'It's only now I know how left behind we were. Some would say twenty, thirty years, I don't know. But even then I was not happy with the way things were. When I was young my dream was to leave the country for good. I decided to leave and not come back. That's how I felt. I was so sick and tired of this place.'

❧ ✿ ✿ ✿ ✿ ✿ ❧

With an easy confidence that comes from not caring too much about what other people think, Darko is comfortable in his skin. But the swagger you might expect from a good-looking lead singer of a rock band isn't there. It seems to me the powerful sense of being left behind has made him a much nicer person than he might otherwise have been. Darko is also smart, self-aware. He recognises his third-world inferiority complex. 'To be a musician from a country like this is difficult. You can only be a follower. You have to choose what you want to be and follow it. For example, if you say your band is a punk band you have to stay typical punk. I have suffered from that. But I want to push myself out. I want to go to the edge, and sometimes I want to cross the line.'

Throughout university and through his early twenties, when Side Effect was starting out, Darko dreamed of leaving Burma. The group had hardly any money, there was nowhere to rehearse and it was difficult and expensive to put on gigs. Band mates were leaving to get 'proper jobs', and Darko sometimes despaired of a musical future. Worst of all was the scrutiny of the military authorities. For all artists, life under army rule was sometimes suffocatingly restrictive. 'I hated some of the shit we had to put up with,' Darko said. Every magazine article, song lyric or album cover had to pass the censor. Knowing that each line they wrote would be examined by a middle-aged government stooge took the edge off their creativity. Darko would take the song lyrics down to the office of the Lyrics Scrutiny and Registration Committee, part of the Myanmar Music Association, itself a department of the Ministry of Culture. Government apparatchiks, sitting among piles of worm-infested scripts, poems and book manuscripts, would check all the words, the design of the cover sleeve, every last thing. Anything that failed to represent the image of a perfect society was removed. There were many examples, such as a line they wrote about buying a cinema ticket on the black market, or the prostitutes working in karaoke bars. They may have scanned well, but they were forbidden. And it wasn't just political dissent the authorities were looking for. Anything rude, any bad language was excised with the stroke of a pen. When your whole reason for being depended on challenging convention, this was a maddening, soul-destroying process. Originality was crushed. One of Darko's friends wrote a song called 'Universal Prophesy', about life, death, but not politics. He was so proud of it. But the censor didn't like it. The word for prophet, *piyadeh*, was considered a religious word and therefore offensive if used in another context. It was cut; the songwriter was distraught. 'Those things build up,' Darko told me. 'Especially when you think you've created something special.'

Censorship has made Burmese popular music more innocent and less challenging than it should be, Darko thinks. 'Burmese bands focus on romantic lyrics because they could pass the censorship. It was so easy and predictable. Some musicians like to think their lyrics are good, but actually, they're shit.' Only one type of music really succeeded in breaking out – hip-hop, which burst on to the Burmese music scene just as the Internet became haphazardly accessible around 2005. Burmese kids embraced it straight away and, happily for them, the youthful vernacular of the rap lyrics seemed to outfox the censors. 'Some of those lyrics, they're so rude, man, I think how did that get through? Then I realised – they used a lot of slang, the censors just didn't get it, they didn't understand. They are old guys. Some people say the lyrics are too rude, but I am happy to hear the fresh lyrics. They are about real feelings, not fake. It's really important to express your real feelings.'

☙ ✿ ✿ ✿ ✿ ✿ ❧

In Burma, parental disapproval is an inhibitor at least as powerful as any law. Darko is from a conventional family. He may be a punk singer but he doesn't dress like a punk – as only a small group do in Burma, with glued Mohicans, ripped denim and piercings. 'For me, being a punk is just a state of mind. But real punks with the punk lifestyle – there are not so many here. To dress up like that is not very easy. Your parents will be upset. That's why it's difficult.' In a culture where family has such a strong influence, Darko's determination to focus on his music has been a test of will. His father, a marine engineer, put pressure on his two sons, Darko and his younger brother Jozeff (Side Effect's guitarist), to pursue more conventional careers. 'Is my father proud of me? Not really. My brother is about to leave the country to become a sailor. We will lose him. He's been listening to the music I like for a long time. He's the good-looking one. It's really hard to find people like him. Now he's going to sea for, like, the rest of his life. The main reason is because of my parents. He's just not as strong as me.'

Interestingly, it was Darko's father who first had the music career. Darko recalls a story he would ask his mother to repeat over and over when he was a child. Before he was born, his dad was a well-known, semi-professional guitar player. The story young Darko liked to hear was that on Rangoon's warm evenings, his neighbours would come out to the street to sit in groups and sip tea. One man would play the acoustic guitar, and others would listen and sing along. But when his father walked down the street, his mother used to tell him, the music would stop. His playing was so revered no one wanted to risk strumming an offbeat chord in front of him. Darko loved that story. 'He had to give up his music to make money and care for his family,' Darko said. 'I feel I have the life he would have wanted.'

If he does, his father won't admit it. His father is still disappointed that his elder son didn't take his advice and study at the military university, a sure-fire route to a cushy life. 'I would get a place to stay, free food, and could become an officer in the army. Later, when you have stars on your shoulders, you can steal the country's money. Even when I was young, I understood the system. I never wanted to do it. The soldiers were the ones who were shooting the kids.'

But a life of principle has not been lucrative. Despite their growing fan base, Darko and the band have made barely any money from their music, and have no illusions that they ever will. They have only occasional opportunities to perform, and those are mostly unpaid or have even left the band in debt, after paying for venues and equipment. So to make a living, Darko and his wife Emily run a men's clothing store in Yuzana Plaza, a giant shopping mall with stationary, clapped-out escalators and frequent power cuts. The business has made them enough money to rent their new apartment nearby, albeit in an embarrassingly bourgeois way. 'It's just a way to pay for our art,' he explains.

☙ ✿ ✿ ✿ ✿ ✿ ❧

I met Emily on my second visit to Darko's flat, late one afternoon, as a thunderstorm brewed outside. Sounds from the street drifted up to the open window, the whir of generators, car horns beeping, urban cockerels crowing at the wrong time of day. Darko and Emily lounged on the sofa opposite me across the glass-topped coffee table with an overflowing ashtray and a vase of plastic flowers. Together for eleven years already, they had nothing on which to model their modern relationship, they made it up as they went along. Emily is a performance artist. The couple share a creative drive and understand each other's struggles.

Emily grew up in a bamboo hut on a scrap of wasteland outside Rangoon. During the sweaty, mosquito-cursed nights, she slept on a woven mat with her parents, three brothers and older sister. There was nothing creative for her. Her parents were poor, and became even poorer when her father died of lung cancer when she was five years old. She missed her father. Not the small income he brought in, just him. She recalled his efforts to bring a little joy to their lives – playing catch with them, growing flowers outside their hut and a monthly trip to the cinema. After his death, Emily's mother sat outside a school all day, selling fried pancakes cooked on a charcoal burner on the side of the road. 'My family was so poor and I didn't have the chance to study art or do it. When I saw my friends doing art classes I told my mother I want to do that too, but the answer was always no.' Art was superfluous, irrelevant to their lives. Emily was expected to do well at school; even for a very poor family, educational achievement was prized as the key to a better life. Success was measured in memorising texts and equations, reciting answers by rote. Self-expression had no value.

Emily met her first boyfriend when she was in ninth grade, although she says it wasn't a physical relationship, more of an innocent crush. Even so, when her elder brothers found out they beat her up badly. They told her she could have a boyfriend only after tenth grade, when she was sixteen. In her final year at school she met Darko. 'I was seventeen and he was nineteen. My family liked him, but they warned me that he would dump me once he had had sex with me. They gave me a hard time, called me names and scolded me every day. Having sex before marriage is not acceptable here. It's dangerous.'

But Darko didn't dump Emily. They dated for years, trying to see each other wherever and whenever they could, while still living with their parents. They suffered the same predicament as many young Burmese couples – they had nowhere to go. On Sunday afternoons, Rangoon's parks and the grassy banks of its lakes are populated by canoodling couples, entwined under trees or on benches by the water. The only way round this is marriage, but that wasn't something Darko and Emily were interested in. Their spirits were free, and they still dreamed of leaving Burma. But, in the end, a wedding was the only option. 'I still don't believe in marriage and all that shit,' Darko explained, making Emily laugh. 'But there's no way we could have moved in together without getting married. Even though we are very free people, in family matters we have to follow convention.' In many ways, Emily said, it was marriage that set her free. 'Getting married has allowed me to become an artist. I couldn't experiment with art, express myself, while I was still living at home. And I couldn't have left home without being married.' She quizzed me on life for young women in the West, intrigued that they were able to leave home alone, move in with friends and boyfriends, support themselves financially. 'In this country, women don't have the money to go and live off their own income. They cannot afford to leave home and parents are happy not to let go of their children. You can stay with them for the rest of your life, and if you bring them grandchildren and great-grandchildren they will be happier still.'

They still try to break the mould. Within a year or two of marriage, a couple is expected to produce a baby, but Darko and Emily have decided to postpone starting a family. They enjoy the freedom of their child-free lives. In the coolness of dusk, they like to take a *passeggiata*, sauntering past teashops with low stools set out on the pavement, and cigarette stands on wheels and packs of ravenous street dogs. They stroll along chatting, their arms casually around each other, a rare sight for a couple in Rangoon.

Emily wanders across the black-and-white chequered lino to shower in the small tiled bathroom with two buckets of water. She returns smelling of citrus and combing her wet hair, having changed into a T-shirt and soft jersey shorts with an elasticated waist, clean and comfortable for an evening in. She is going to show me a DVD called *Distortion*, one of her performance art pieces. Emily is round-faced, unthreatening; there is little about her to suggest the power of her artistic expression. 'I have a split personality,' she says. 'When I am performing I feel like a different person.'

The DVD was filmed in the Lokanat Gallery in central Rangoon, a wide, open space with high ceilings, huge open windows and a blue and terracotta Victorian tiled floor. The gallery is housed in a neo-classical building with a Florentine dome built in the late nineteenth century by a Baghdadi Jewish trader. Once one of the city's most prestigious business addresses, greyish green mould now seeps across its faded mustard exterior. Much of the building is deserted, except for a family of six who live in the metal-caged lift shaft.

Rangoon's artistic community and some interested foreigners had gathered for Emily's performance, standing around the edge of the room. It was 15 August 2010; Aung San Suu Kyi was still in detention and Burma still under General Than Shwe's control. Prior to the performance, Emily had to give a preview to the inspectors from the Ministry of Culture. A panel of middle-aged men, one of them absent-mindedly picking his teeth with a cocktail stick after lunch, listened to her outline her plans for the avant-garde piece. 'It was so totally embarrassing' she said. 'How could I begin to explain what I wanted to do?'

We watch the DVD together. Emily is wearing a black shirt and trousers, an apron and a gauzy black blindfold that she seems to be able to see through. She has laid a neat, low table in the centre of the room with a tablecloth, four bowls and china cups. She takes a handful of spoons and gives one to each person in the audience 'Then they'll think, "What's going to happen, will I be asked to join in?" They probably think it will be something nice.'

She squats down at the table with the ease of a Burmese woman well practised at sitting on her haunches. She lights four candles and sets them out carefully around the place settings. She reaches into her bag and pulls out white tissue paper, which she rips up, putting a handful in each bowl. She takes a cigarette lighter and sets light to each pile of tissue paper, so that each bowl contains a small blaze. There is a murmur in the audience. Emily is focused. She lets the bowls burn for a few seconds, then turns around, picks up a baseball bat and rains blows on the table, smashing up the china bowls and cups, her destruction timed perfectly as the tissue paper burns itself out, leaving the table strewn with shattered, smoking rubble. She breathes out, turns to the audience and bows.

'After I finished my performance I felt really grateful, really light. It's hard to find venues to do this sort of thing. It's not normal in Burma. Of course I couldn't just do that sort of thing anywhere, like in the street. We'd be totally screwed if we tried to do that.'

✿ ✿ ✿ ✿ ✿ ✿

'Why are we still here?' They laugh. They complain about the excruciatingly slow Internet connection, petty corruption and frequent power cuts. 'It's the same old shit,' Darko says. But despite their youthful dreams of fleeing Burma, Darko and Emily seem happy where they are, comfortable on home turf and inspired within their close group of artistic friends. Burma is starting to change, they are discovering new freedoms and opportunities, and at last Rangoon feels like a city of possibilities. Is that why they have stayed? In fact, it is for a deeper reason. As for many young Burmese, the Saffron Revolution of 2007, and the government's violent crackdown, was a turning point in Darko's life. It made him see, with new, sharp clarity, what his country was really like, and what it really needed.

In September 2007, Darko and his friends had joined one of the street protests. It had felt safe: day by day the protests had grown bigger, and the involvement of thousands of monks seemed to have lent the demonstrators a protective shield. But then the crackdown began. Darko and his friends had left the main march and were walking together through a quiet part of town. A truck of soldiers drove into the street and started shooting; later he found out they were rubber bullets. 'But they weren't demonstrators on the streets, they were just people from the streets,' he said, still confused and disturbed by the memory. 'I didn't mean to run. I just ran. We all ran into a building, up the stairs. We were banging on doors, begging people to let us into their apartments. One minute we were heroes, marching along, shouting slogans. But then we were really scared. Very quickly.'

From their vantage point they could see a boy who worked in a teashop. The soldiers approached him. One soldier picked up a stool and hit him hard round the head. He fell down, blood seeping from a cut on his forehead. 'We were watching from the top of the stairs. We were shaking. He was sent to the hospital. We wanted to tell them that he was just the boy from the teashop.' A woman walked down the street, carrying a small basket on her way to the market. 'Get on the ground, get on the ground!' yelled one of the soldiers, pointing a rifle in her face. She started to kneel down but, as she did so, she tried to explain to the soldiers that she was just going to the bazaar. A mistake. The soldier slapped her round the face. 'We could hear that slap from the top of the building,' Darko said. 'She fell on the ground. The soldiers screamed at her. "Don't talk unless I ask you!"' Bearing witness to this brutality, this injustice, changed Darko's mindset for good. 'I changed my mind about leaving,' he said. 'I decided to do something for this country. We are not politicians, but what we can do best is be artists. We need good musicians, good poets, good painters. Before that day I was trying to leave my country as soon as possible, but then I realised something. I couldn't desert this place. This country needs people like me.'

☆☆☆☆☆

Ironically, it was only after Darko had made his decision to stay in Burma that the opportunities to travel abroad actually came up. In 2007, the idea that Side Effect would perform abroad was unimaginable. But five years later, as Burma started to emerge from its cultural hibernation, the band received its first international invitation – to play at an indie music festival in Bali, Indonesia. They played on the same billing as legendary Bali punk band Superman is Dead, and made enough money to buy a drum set for Tser Htoo, and release their debut album *Rainy Night Dreams*.

Next, two documentary makers, Alexander Dluzak and Carsten Piefke, came to Rangoon to make a film about the Burmese punk scene and left with a plan to bring Side Effect to Germany. In December 2012,

Darko, Jozeff and Tser Htoo landed in snowy Berlin. It was their first experience of freezing weather, twinkly Christmas lights and short, frosty winter days. They survived wearing borrowed long johns and eating pizza. Two gigs were planned, one at a small club in Hamburg and the second at a big venue in Berlin. Darko loved playing to a more sophisticated audience than he was used to. 'In Burma the sound is still quite new to people. It doesn't fit into their categories and they don't know how to react.' In Berlin, the crowd was bouncing from the first beat. When the band played their English-language song 'Change' they were wild, some were even stage diving. Darko could hardly believe it was happening. 'It was dreamlike, magical,' he told me. 'We felt like we were in a movie.'

The filmmakers had lent them an apartment, but the band had arrived with virtually no money. They just didn't have any. 'We would go into the shop, we didn't know what to buy, so we just bought frozen pizza every day and put it in the oven. There was a pain in my stomach the whole time. The others were even worse. They just couldn't stop thinking about rice.' The Berlin experience reinforced Darko's love of home, his need to be there, and not just for the food. 'We've realised that this is not like the music scene in the rest of the world. If we were a band in New York City or Berlin we would be just like hundreds of others. Here there is no one else. This city needs Side Effect. I want to show people here that they can have the same things too.'

❧ ✿ ✿ ✿ ✿ ✿ ☙

Just after his thirty-second birthday, Darko is reclining on his sofa, resting his bandaged, broken right foot. He's desperately hoping that the outer metatarsal heals before Side Effect's next planned trip to Berlin and Copenhagen in the summer. The fracture was caused by a few too many Jägermeisters before a gig, followed by an ill-advised onstage leap. Darko is flossing his teeth as he speaks; he has recently given up his packet-a-day smoking habit. ('Easy,' he says.) Emily pops back briefly from the shop in Yuzana Plaza. She has a big order for some brown military-style security guard uniforms and needs the photograph to show her seamstress. Things are changing in Burma, but most of the time things don't seem dramatically different for Darko and Emily. They are chronically short of money. 'You wanna know about everyday life?' Darko vented in a Facebook post, 'Quick answer is fucking boring. If boiling hot weather amuses you, that's fine. If seeing poor people working the whole day for low income makes you feel amazing, that's okay. If talking with closed-minded people makes you feel like a wise man, no problem. But I'm not okay. I'm stuck and fucked up.'

Of course Darko isn't satisfied. He is a punk after all. He sees the beginning of a new Burma, some small steps. He no longer has to submit his lyrics to the censor board, and Emily doesn't need pre-approval for her performances. There is a long way to go, Darko believes. To make his point, he hoists himself up from the couch, hobbles towards me on his steel crutch, pulls up a stool and lifts his leg with two hands to rest his broken foot beside me. He is sitting very close. 'Freedom means continuing to fight. In the new Burma there are still a lot of things to fight for. They are still the same guys, right? They just took off their uniforms and got another place in power. We can't be fucking happy till they're gone.'

# 14
# New Realities

I stepped out of the airport doors into the familiar embrace of Rangoon's heavy, musty air. Above the taxi rank was a dot matrix display board, confirming the fares to various parts of town. New. I was already starting to lose count of the new things I had noted since I landed forty minutes ago. First the plane was crowded with tourists: middle-aged American couples in Rohan pants and sensible sandals with velcro closures, young German backpackers with ankle tattoos, a Chinese tour party with too much carry-on baggage and brand-new YSL handbags purchased in Bangkok. New. No nerves at the immigration counter. New. Two money exchange counters near the baggage carousels offering competitive rates. New. (Gone was the official counter that used to offer a kyat-dollar conversion more than a hundred times lower than the black-market rate.) Through customs (no more worries about whether they would search my bag, find something incriminating on my laptop) to a counter where I could hire my own mobile phone and SIM card at a very reasonable rate. New. (There was still no international roaming service in Burma, hence the need for a rented phone, but I was far from disappointed – my expectations of communications technology in Burma were extremely low).

Outside there was a line of pristine, white, air-conditioned Toyota taxis and minivans, all with their engines purring, waiting for fares. But when I reached the head of the queue and my cab crawled up, I saw with nostalgia it was an early 1980s, decrepit old banger. I sank into the saggy dampness of the back seat, feeling like I was back in the old days, until – again – I saw something new. In front of me on the dashboard was a collage of stickers – portraits of the Lady, her father and the peacock emblem of her National League for Democracy party. Two red NLD flags on little cocktail sticks were stuck to the top of the rear-view mirror. The driver looked back at me in the reflection.

'Do you like our Lady?' he asked, smiling.

'Er, yes,' I hesitated, looking back at him, worriedly. Was that the right answer? Was it a trick? Only two years ago, just whispering Aung

San Suu Kyi's name, even an oblique reference, would have been dangerous. A disgruntled taxi driver might risk a generic 'life is difficult' to convey his dissatisfaction with military rule, but many would have been uncomfortable even with that. 'Yes, Burma very good,' they would say, with a bitter laugh. Now the once-banned image of the opposition leader was adorning my driver's car. What's more, I saw, as we rumbled into town, windows down, that her face was everywhere, on posters pasted to walls and on T-shirts sold from street stalls at every junction.

In a city that had been sealed tight and preserved for decades in mouldering isolation, the signs of change were everywhere. My face at the open window, already covered in a gritty scum from the wet, diesely air, I mentally itemised what was new as we dodged through traffic on Insein Road; a steel-and-glass apartment building at eight-mile junction; an ATM machine built into the side of the shopping centre; a row of neo-classical mansions a half-mile further down the road which had been abandoned mid-construction, now complete and inhabited. We turned down Parami Road with new kerbstones and walkable pavements and a windowless breeze-block building bearing the sign 'Public Toilet'. Along Kabar Aye Pagoda Road we passed the Sedona Hotel, with its ugly façade of faux-traditional tiered roofs and towers, the vista that greeted Aung San Suu Kyi each day through her years in captivity in her house across the lake. We crossed the junction and there was a hole in the skyline. What was there before? I couldn't remember. Whatever it was had been demolished, and the site was cordoned off by corrugated-iron hoardings, ready for redevelopment. We turned right across the traffic into the lane that led us to Golden Valley. On one side of the road was an empty space where once stood my favourite Rangoon store, certainly the most picturesque: a blue, classic VW combi van, stacked up on bricks, one wing removed, selling bananas, baskets of mangos in season, cigarettes, coffee mix and dried noodles. One of the nicest by-products of Rangoon's time capsule economy was the city's fleet of fabulous vintage cars, including sleek 1960s Mercedes and the smiling VW vans.

✿ ✿ ✿ ✿ ✿

It was September 2013 and I was back in Rangoon to teach a week-long journalism course held at a diplomats' club with a clear blue swimming pool and neatly tended garden. The smell of fried food lingered in the dining room: fish and chips and pie and mash were mainstays of the menu. A former diplomat pitched up at the club at eleven every morning, sweating from his hot car journey, and ordered a Myanmar Beer. Excited by Burma's nascent economic reforms, he had quit his diplomatic career to set up a business consultancy with his Burmese wife, to advise twenty-first-century prospectors on how best to make a buck out of the new Burma. He didn't have an office yet, so he had set up a workspace next to the bar.

Unsure about how open we could be in this fast-changing nation, the course organisers had chosen a safe venue and we had worried that the young Burmese participants would be nervous about talking politics. But the journalists quickly pointed out our misconceptions about what was holding back their freedom of speech: 'We can say what we like on the Internet, it's just that we can't afford to use it!' They arrived an hour early each day to take advantage of the free Wi-Fi and coffee. Most of them in their early twenties, they talked as if the big news landmarks of the last quarter century – the 1988 uprising, the 1996 student revolt, the Saffron Revolution of 2007 – were just notes in history; they seemed ready to move on. At an end-of-course drinks party at the same panoramic restaurant where I had nervously interviewed the former prisoner Win Tin, I met the respected Burmese author and newspaper editor U Pe Myint. He wore a formal apricot-coloured jacket over a white shirt, and ankle-length *longyi*. I told him about the confidence of the young journalists, their high expectations. 'Those of us who are older have felt so many disappointments, it's hard for us to feel like this. But the young people don't feel it. They don't know how it feels to be disappointed.'

The next afternoon I had the novel experience of asking the driver of a taxi I flagged down on the street to take me to the NLD offices on Shwegondine Road. I felt no fear, and he exhibited no surprise: the crowded, ramshackle offices of Aung San Suu Kyi's party had become a magnet for foreign tourists. They were unlikely to catch a glimpse of the Lady herself, who now spent most of her time in Naypyidaw as a sitting MP and had drastically cut down her media interviews and public appearances. But visitors were at least able to stock up on NLD kitsch – stickers, key chains, mugs and T-shirts, bearing the Lady's image or the peacock emblem of her party.

The military intelligence agents, once a constant presence across the road, were gone. People moved freely in and out of the offices, which had changed little since my last visit: peeling walls, creaking fans, images of Suu Kyi gazing down from every wall. The hot downstairs room was full to bursting, despite the new overspill premises the party had leased next door. Informal committee meetings were convened at trestle tables, a photography exhibition was being set up at the back. I looked for Peter, the young NLD volunteer with whom I had chatted while waiting to interview Suu Kyi. He wasn't around, but plenty of other young party members were – fresh blood for what had once been an ageing party. The NLD's technologically savvy twenty-somethings had established a new research unit, an attempt perhaps to decentralise power from Suu Kyi, for whom the transition from dissident democracy heroine to a working politician had not been an easy one.

Once above scrutiny and criticism, Aung San Suu Kyi had been accused by some of her supporters of aloofness and reluctance to delegate. While her party had enjoyed runaway success in the 2012 by-election, some of its younger members were frustrated by their leader's lack of interest in technology and failure to modernise the party in preparation to fight the 2015 general election, a vote that could propel their once downtrodden movement into government for the first time. Even her stance on more fundamental issues rankled her supporters. As a general's daughter, Suu Kyi made a habit of voicing her fondness for the Burmese army, a sentiment that some of her fellow former political prisoners, slower to forgive their military jailers, found perplexing. Human rights campaigners, traditionally her devoted allies, were exasperated by her inexplicably muted comments on religious intolerance and the persecution of minorities.

Many of Suu Kyi's once adoring followers may have found her behaviour baffling, but she was treading a delicate line. The Nobel peace laureate was Burma's most popular politician, but according to the country's constitution could not become its president. The 2008 charter, imposed in a farcical referendum held in the aftermath of Cyclone Nargis, barred from the presidency anyone with a foreign spouse or children. As the widow of British scholar Michael Aris, and the mother of two sons who held British passports, Suu Kyi could have been forgiven for believing this clause in the constitution specifically targeted her. Amending the constitution required the support of some of the same generals with whom she had fought for so long. The document guaranteed military appointees a quarter of seats in parliament, and, ensuring the army's continued power, stipulated that the votes of more than three-quarters of parliamentarians were needed to make any amendments. It could hardly be described as a charter for democracy. Suu Kyi, while famous for her principled, uncompromising resistance to injustice, liked to emphasise that she was a politician, not an icon. 'Icons don't actually do anything,' she had told me. Out of detention, she was in the tougher, real world of politics. Reforming the constitution, clearing a path to the presidency, and breaking the military's long grip on power in Burma was a prize for which it seemed she had decided compromise might be necessary.

※ ☆ ☆ ☆ ☆ ※

The mood at Shwedagon pagoda serves as a useful barometer in unpredictable times. Bearing witness silently above the city, the golden bell-shaped stupa holds an indefinable authority. The pagoda, each day lovingly regilded with leaves of gold, is some five hundred years old in its existing form, and archaeologists believe it shelters yet more ancient structures. Some things are constant – the streams of quiet pilgrims, lotus flowers in hand, fervently praying. Some things are not. The first time I visited, the day after the violent crackdown on the Saffron Uprising, it was gun-toting soldiers, not red-robed monks, who sat in the shade of its jewel-encrusted shrines. But today, old and young, rich and poor are here. It is the place to go to take the pulse of the nation.

I arrived at the eastern gate at close to dusk, signed in (for the first time using my own name), paid my foreigner's fee, removed my shoes and ascended the covered staircase to the shrine, lined either side with stalls selling little brass bells, papier-mâché animals, jade bangles and painted silk parasols. I chatted to one of the tour guides on my way up. Visitor numbers had doubled, tripled in the last year, he told me, now there was no low season, even in the monsoon rains. A family skipped up the stairs past me, two young children chasing each other and laughing, holding paper flowers on sticks as they tried to take the steps two at a time.

I circumambulated the stupa in a clockwise direction, the marble floor warm under my feet. Children playfully gonged the giant brass bells with heavy wooden clubs. Worshippers poured water over the heads of small Buddha statues representing the day of the week on which they were born, and adorned them with strings of jasmine. In front of each shrine men and women knelt alone, genuflecting, absorbed in prayer. Halfway round, I saw a new ATM machine in the blue, white and red colours of the bank, plonked incongruously next to a mosaiced shrine. I used to bring months of money into the country in crisp, hundred-dollar bills; now, if I ran short, extra kyats were waiting to be disgorged right here inside the temple. Grey clouds gathered above us, a dramatic, swirling backdrop to the gleaming stupa. Smoky infernos of slim white candles burned as daylight started to fade. I descended the staircase back to the gate. To the side, next to a small fishpond, was a marble-floored area with a plastic picnic table and chairs. Two monks were sitting cross-legged on the floor, each with a bare shoulder hunched over as they read. On the chairs sat two men and an elderly woman, feet bare, her grey hair pinned back, in intense concentration as she read from the newspaper in front of her.

This was another of Rangoon's new phenomena. Shwedagon used to be a place of whispers, where monks would latch on to foreigners as they toured the pagoda, with the excuse of wanting to practise their English, answering furtively delivered questions about life in Burma and making their own inquiries about life in the West. They were often naïve, insubstantial exchanges, but the monks were eager for knowledge and tourists relished these unscripted encounters with 'real people'. Inside Burma, information was suppressed – restricted to the heavily censored, often mendacious output sanctioned by the state.

By this September evening, all censorship before publication had been lifted. An array of privately owned, newly licensed daily newspapers were available to all those who could afford to buy them. To encourage the sharing of information, the trustees of Shwedagon had established a small newspaper library at the foot of the pagoda, which they called 'Twilight Reading'. Dozens of papers and journals were delivered each evening, with an archive going back several months. Worshippers would descend the steps after evening prayers to read the day's news. The library was set above a bus interchange; other visitors were commuters who would spend an hour or so leafing through the newsprint, sitting out the rush hour before heading home. It was a simple concept, but for the readers, quietly absorbing each unexpurgated article, it was an undreamed-of freedom.

❧ ✿ ✿ ✿ ✿ ✿ ❧

Breathlessly dubbed 'Asia's last frontier', Burma was experiencing something of a gold rush. Following Barack Obama's visit in November 2012, US and European Union sanctions on Burma were relaxed. Investors were rushing in to grab their share of this almost virgin market of more than fifty million people. 'There is a feeling that this is the last great adventure there may be in South-east Asia,' the chief executive of an Asian real-estate firm told the Bloomberg news agency. On cream leather couches in the lobby of the Park Royal, a modern, five-star business hotel (where once vacant rooms were now booked up six months ahead), clutches of foreign executives, coffees or beers in front of them, tapped on their smartphones and laptops. A Canadian friend of mine, an NGO worker in his mid-twenties, was walking through the foyer one morning on the way to the conference room on the far side. 'I was stopped three times: Are you Brad? Are you Jeff? Are you Nick? It was crazy. They're all looking for their fixers.'

My Burmese Facebook friends faithfully documented each new piece of evidence that proved Burma was joining the global economy. They posted photos of themselves swigging the first legally imported Coca-Colas, making peace signs outside Burma's first KFC restaurant, posing in an electronics store next to a boxed, cellophane-wrapped Samsung Galaxy S3. When I was living in Rangoon, there was a billboard featuring a young couple in fluffy white bathrobes snuggled in front of a MacBook Pro. I did a double take when I first saw it – there were no international brands in Burma – until I realised it was actually an advertisement for coffee powder. Now the international brands were here, a new one landing every week.

The surge in investment interest was putting pressure on the city's real-estate market. A desperate shortage of office space, hotel rooms and executive housing had pushed rents in parts of downtown Rangoon up to $100 per square foot, higher than many properties in Manhattan. The city was enjoying – or enduring – a construction boom. At every turn there seemed to be a new gap in the cityscape, like the one I had seen as I drove in from the airport. Downtown plots were boarded off, foundations dug, new high-rises set to sprout. Plans were laid for luxury hotels, shiny shopping malls and towering office blocks. The same Facebook friends who posted photos of the latest consumer brands shared their concerns about the pace of redevelopment. They knew the military government's long neglect of Rangoon had not only brought the misery of blackouts, potholed streets, uncollected rubbish and overloaded buses; it had also preserved the city's historic charm, a wealth of eclectic architecture without parallel in South-east Asia. For every Facebook photo of a new gadget, there was an affectionate picture of a peeling, pale green Victorian-era tenement block with laundry strung up on fretwork balconies, the spires of St Mary's Cathedral from an office window, a field of patched-up corrugated iron roofs with the turreted Secretariat in the background, and dozing trishaw drivers in front of the lilac City Hall. In this wild-west landscape of rapid change, Rangoon's stately, mildewed heart – the grand backdrop to coups, assassinations and protests, and home to the messy intimacies of city life – was under threat.

✤ ✤ ✤ ✤ ✤ ✤ ✤

The prospect of unbridled, greedy development was not the only dark side to Burma's reforms. Something else was new in Rangoon. Everywhere I went, I noticed a new symbol. Postcard-sized stickers were pasted in shop windows, on noodle wagons and teashop tables. The stickers looked innocuous enough – a patchwork of pastel stripes, overlain with a yellow chakra wheel and '969' written in Burmese numerals. I soon discovered that '969' was a Buddhist nationalist movement which had appeared following the reforms of 2011 and rapidly gained the support of many of Burma's majority Buddhists. The 969 movement's populist, conspiratorial message, depicting a Buddhist society under attack, was disseminated quickly by social media, pamphlets and DVDs, finding an eager constituency among those with an appetite for blame and fuelling anti-Muslim rhetoric. The loosening of authoritarian control can always, it seems, give rise to unexpected consequences. In Burma, new freedoms had rekindled old animosities and prejudices that military rule had appeared to keep in check.

# 15
# 969

It was Maung Maung Myint who organised his high school reunion, keen to revive memories of happy days at Thingangyun State High School No 3. From the class of 1971, some had done well in life, among them lawyers, an airline pilot and a lieutenant general. Maung Maung Myint, a youthful-looking fifty-eight-year-old, proudly handed me a glossy photograph of their recent reunion, the alumni seated on the floor of the meeting hall he had chosen, those deemed most successful at the front, the former classmates creased up with laughter from a joke that had just been told. The photograph showed Maung Maung Myint sitting cross-legged on the carpet in the centre of the front row. He had shining black eyes and the widest smile of all.

Maung Maung Myint's grandparents had arrived in cosmopolitan, British-ruled Rangoon in the 1920s, a young Muslim couple from Chittagong in the Raj's Eastern Bengal province, chasing dreams and opportunities in the thriving port city with its imposing buildings, tree-lined boulevards and smooth-running network of electric streetcars. They were part of a massive, early twentieth-century wave of immigration to Burma from all across British India – both Hindus and Muslims from Madras to Karachi. Many came to serve in the colonial administration, and with them came doctors, merchants, moneylenders and street sweepers.

Dominating Rangoon's skyline was Shwedagon pagoda, the sacred emblem of Burma's majority faith, Buddhism. But the newly-weds from Bengal did not feel excluded – they had arrived in a city with every major religion represented: Catholic and Anglican cathedrals, a synagogue on 26th Street, Hindu temples, and a good collection of mosques. They felt comfortable strolling along the shaded, swept pavements of the downtown streets where they would rub shoulders with Buddhist monks, Scottish solicitors and Greek traders. On the waterfront promenade on Strand Road they would sit on a bench, she in a bright headscarf, he in a *longyi* and collarless white shirt, to watch the steam ships dock, liners en route to London or Shanghai.

Maung Maung Myint's grandfather began to pray at the Bengali Sunni Jameh mosque, built in 1862 on the north side of the traffic circle that also housed the ancient Sule Pagoda, a busy Buddhist temple. Across the road, in front of the red-brick High Court, a twin-spired Baptist church was under construction, funded by donations from American ministries. As Indian migrants continued to arrive, seeking their fortunes in the frontier-land of Burma, the mosque's congregation grew rapidly. With guidance from his fellow worshippers, the young Bengali set about establishing a small enterprise, an import–export business for beans and pulses. With their first child on the way, the couple found a small apartment to rent in a newly built, freshly painted tenement block on 30th Street. Rangoon, a jewel of the British Empire, was a bustling, optimistic place, and Maung Maung Myint's grandparents felt part of its future already.

☙ ✿ ✿ ✿ ✿ ✿ ❧

Half a century later, their grandson was the only Muslim in his class at high school in a northern Rangoon suburb. His parents, born in Rangoon, had given their children Burmese names, but never tried to hide or downplay their Islamic faith. Maung Maung Myint was a popular pupil, known not only in his class but by everyone in the school. He didn't mind being the outsider, the odd one out, he said, his friends always made it easy for him. 'My school days were the best days,' he smiled, giving the impression of someone for whom nothing that followed ever matched the camaraderie of his teenage years. Did he feel different from his friends? 'Buddhists and Muslims had a very good relationship. There was no problem between us. At Eid, my Buddhist friends would bring me food as a gift. At *Thingyan* (Burmese New Year) we would celebrate together. And today, among my friends, things are still the same.'

Like his grandparents, Maung Maung Myint was an optimist. When talking to me, he seemed to stretch every sinew to find hope amid the poisonous sectarian atmosphere that permeated the Burma of 2013. The loosening of the regime's grip had provided a new outlet for extremist voices. Communal violence first broke out in Arakan state on the Bay of Bengal at the start of the 2012 rains. Sparked by the rape and murder of a Buddhist woman by Muslim men, Buddhist mobs went on the rampage, killing dozens of Muslims, and setting light to their mosques, businesses and homes. Violence flared again in October of that year, forcing tens of thousands of Muslim Rohingyas to flee their homes. Over the following months the violence spread, years of latent resentment boiling over into riots and massacres. In March 2013, in the central town of Meiktila, a heated argument between a Muslim jeweller and his Buddhist customer over a broken gold clip quickly escalated. Angry crowds thronged around the shop, dividing their allegiance along religious lines. A false rumour spread that the customer had died from her injuries after being attacked by the shopkeeper. Anti-Muslim gangs set about ransacking the gold shops of the market area; in revenge Muslim men knocked a Buddhist monk off his motorbike, beat him and stabbed him to death. The murder unleashed a three-day killing spree of Muslims – a thousand-strong Buddhist mob, armed with knives and iron bars, rampaged through town in a raging frenzy, unrestrained by police or any security forces. They killed more than forty Muslims, burned down hundreds of homes and Muslim-owned shops, and razed five mosques.

The clashes seemed to be contagious, erupting in the market town of Lashio in the Shan hills, in Okkan in Lower Burma and in Thandwe, the gateway to many of Burma's most beautiful beaches. But aside from some minor disputes and skirmishes, Rangoon had mainly escaped the violence when I sat opposite Maung Maung Myint on the cool, cream marble floor of the downtown mosque where his grandfather used to pray. Maung Maung Myint, who now ran the family's pulse and bean business, was general secretary of the mosque and a respected leader of Rangoon's 300,000-strong Muslim community. 'Let us hope for the best,' he said, with a tight smile, running his fingers lightly over the photographs of his Buddhist classmates on the floor between us, as if seeking reassurance that the bonds of friendship were still real and strong. 'Among my friends, nothing has changed. Nothing has changed.'

But Maung Maung Myint knew the landscape had shifted, and he was nervous. The previous week an argument had broken out in his neighbourhood, a scenario similar to the dispute in Meiktila that triggered such terrible violence. Just after evening prayers Maung Maung Myint received a text message on the little Nokia phone he kept in a leather holster on his waist, urging him to come back quickly to his home suburb of Tamwe. Two women had got into a fight, a crowd had gathered and it looked like things could escalate. A Buddhist customer had accused a Muslim shopkeeper of short-changing her in her weekly purchase of rice and spices. 'She said the quality wasn't good. The shopkeeper said everything was the same as usual, she said her customer was just looking for a fight.' It was eight o'clock in the evening by the time he arrived. The power was out, as it often was, and the night was inky black. He took aside some of his young nephews, told them to make sure the Muslim women and children in the neighbourhood were at home, behind locked doors. Then he set about defusing the argument, negotiating between the two women in an atmosphere of excruciating tension and rising hostility. Five hours later he returned home, having gently resolved the dispute to the grudging satisfaction of both sides. He sat down at the kitchen table, head in his trembling hands, exhausted. His eighty-five-year-old mother, his wife and his daughter had been waiting up for him behind their bolted apartment door. His wife put the kettle on the stove, and lit the gas with a match. 'I didn't sleep after that,' he said. 'It was life or death.'

✿ ✿ ✿ ✿ ✿ ✿

Muslims account for between 4 and 8 per cent of the population in overwhelmingly Buddhist Burma. The figures are disputed. Community leaders say the Muslim population is at the higher end of that range, but the government does not recognise Muslims as an official minority, so the statistics are difficult to verify. While their numbers swelled dramatically in the colonial era, the Muslim presence in Burma predates the British occupation. Islamic influence stretches back centuries – the fifteenth-century Arakanese kings in Mrauk-U encouraged a mixed Buddhist–Muslim court, and in the nineteenth century, King Mindon, a devout Buddhist, defended and supported Mandalay's large Muslim community. Today, Muslim communities are scattered all over the country, with their biggest concentrations in Arakan, now known as Rakhine, and Rangoon. But while Maung Maung Myint was loath to admit it, the image of Buddhists and Muslims living harmoniously side by side for years was not an accurate reflection of history. Enmity towards Muslims was rooted in the mass migration of the colonial period, of which Maung Maung Myint's grandparents were a part. The steady stream of immigration from the mid-nineteenth century reached a flow of nearly half a million per year by the late 1920s. The influx of both Hindus and Muslims from across the subcontinent was unchecked, even encouraged, by Burma's British occupiers, stirring fear and resentment among the native Burmese.

During the Great Depression of the 1930s, the *Chettyar* moneylenders from southern India were hated caricatures. The main source of credit for desperate rice farmers suffering the collapse of global prices, they laid claim to vast tracts of mortgaged land when their debtors defaulted. In the docks of Rangoon, unskilled Indian workers took jobs that were once the preserve of Burmese, and a 1930 strike by Indian dockers led to a dispute that fuelled deadly anti-Indian riots. In 1938, the publication of a book by a Muslim author that allegedly contained material offensive to Buddhists sparked another wave of bloody sectarian clashes. The 1930s marked the height of the Indian presence in Burma; during the Second World War, around half a million members of the Indian community in Burma fled the invading Japanese army, most of them trekking on foot through rain forest to Assam. And from 1964, hundreds of thousands of immigrants from the subcontinent were expelled by General Ne Win to India and Pakistan, a dramatic, forced exodus much greater than Idi Amin's expulsion of Ugandan Asians, but one that was barely noted in history.

Despite their depleted numbers, hostility towards Muslims bubbled under the surface during Burma's long years of military rule. Freedom of expression was restrained, but ill feeling had not evaporated. It flared up in occasional outbreaks of violence, such as the anti-Muslim riots, which erupted in the usually sedate port city of Moulmein in 1983, forcing hundreds of Muslim families to flee across the border to Thailand. In 1997, a Buddhist mob in Mandalay attacked mosques and Muslim businesses, and in 2001, when the Taliban blew up the ancient Bamiyan Buddhas in Afghanistan, angry Buddhists in the Burmese town of Taungoo exacted revenge on their Muslim neighbours. But the Muslim group that suffered most under the rule of the generals was the Rohingya of Arakan state. In a country infamous for mistreating its own citizens, the Rohingya, who number some 800,000, have long been at the bottom of the heap, their persecution unmatched possibly anywhere in the world.

Rohingya leaders say they have lived in Arakan, a strip of land along the Indian Ocean and close to the border with Bangladesh, for centuries. Indeed, evidence of a Muslim population in the territory, which in its heyday was a wealthy centre of trade and scholarship, dates back hundreds of years. But Burma's military government, and the civilian-led administration that followed, claimed that most of the Rohingya – an Islamic people darker skinned than most Burmese – were in fact recent immigrants from Bangladesh. Following the coup of 1962, Ne Win's regime introduced policies that denied citizenship status to the majority of the Rohingya people. Their lives, already blighted by poverty, became increasingly intolerable. A large Tatmadaw contingent was deployed to Arakan, and soldiers confiscated land, levied arbitrary taxes and imposed forced labour on villages. The Rohingya suffered daily humiliations, with every aspect of their lives, from marriage to education, tightly controlled. If a Rohingya man wanted to travel from one village to another, even a distance of a few miles, he had first to obtain a permit from the local SPDC office. Rohingyas needed permission to marry that would cost several months' wages in bribes and could take many years. Young Rohingyas faced discrimination at school from both Buddhist Arakanese students and their teachers, and even the brightest pupils were barred from studying the most prestigious subjects at university, such as medicine or engineering. Thanks to the brutality of the pogroms against the Rohingya and their desperate escape bids on rickety boats across the Indian Ocean, the plight of these stateless people has received considerable media attention and their treatment has drawn rebuke from foreign governments. By late 2013, around 140,000 Rohingya were living in desperate conditions in squalid camps, their homes either destroyed or too unsafe to return to. Their children were dying of malnutrition and disease. Troublingly, the persecution of the Rohingya seemed to be blithely accepted on the streets of Rangoon, even among the most educated and well informed. 'Those *kalars*,' one bright young masters student and Fulbright candidate told me, 'they are dogs. I hate them.'

~ ✿ ✿ ✿ ✿ ✿ ~

Maung Maung Myint led me up a wooden staircase with a heavily lacquered banister to the roof of the mosque. We stepped out into the hot glare of the afternoon, the western sun glinting off the golden stupa of Sule Pagoda, a stone's throw away. Loudspeakers set in the arched windows of the mosque's blue-and-white-tiled minaret were trained on the speakers on the roof of the pagoda, just metres apart. Beyond that, slightly fuzzy in the afternoon haze, were the slim white spires of St Emmanuel's Church. Maung Maung Myint looked out at the view, little changed from the vista his grandfather had enjoyed in the late 1920s. The fusion of the muezzin's call, the chant of Buddhist sutras and the peal of church bells, overlain with the rumble of traffic and diesel generators, was the comforting soundtrack to Maung Maung Myint's life. 'We have good relations with the pagoda. They use their loudspeaker; we use ours. There have never been complaints between us, never one problem,' he said wistfully.

But down on the street, the proliferation of the brightly coloured 969 stickers told a different story. The 969 movement's figurehead was the softly spoken Buddhist monk Wirathu. With his cherubic face, and toothy, childish smile, the militant preacher delivered his sermons on the Islamic peril afflicting Burma in a soporific monotone. A central narrative of his rhetoric was the contention that Muslim men were not only stealing jobs and resources that rightfully belonged to Buddhists, but were chasing Buddhist women too, diluting the purity of Burmese Buddhist blood. In a country still blighted by poverty, where most had yet to feel any economic benefit of the country's opening, Wirathu's proffering of a scapegoat found resonance. He urged Buddhists to boycott Muslim shops and restaurants and to shun interfaith marriages. Followers of his campaign to vilify Islam, ever growing in number, looked for the 969 stickers on the doors of businesses – an assurance that the owners were Buddhist. Muslims found they were no longer welcome in their favourite teashop or at the corner store, and were aghast to find their own shops and enterprises shedding customers in droves.

Sitting cross-legged under a slowly beating fan, Maung Maung Myint claimed to be unperturbed by 969, this highly visible manifestation of ill-feeling towards Muslims. 'I have no feelings about it. I still go into the same shops, and buy mohinga or whatever I feel like. I don't care about 969. If a taxi has a 969 sticker, I just ignore it. I choose the one that will give me the cheapest fare, I get in and I say nothing.' 969 professed to be a non-violent movement, but its hate speech echoed the racist rhetoric that accompanied the worst mass atrocities of the twentieth century, playing to the poorest and least educated at the very bottom of society. Maung Maung Myint believed poverty was powering extremism. 'The people don't have jobs. The cronies have all the money. Many Muslims work hard, they have small businesses, they are not rich but they get by. People see that and they are jealous.' The downtown, the better-off part of Rangoon, had been spared violence, he noted, but skirmishes had already broken out in the impoverished quarters of Kungyangon, Shwepyithar and Thaketa. 'It's simple. Wages are low and prices are going up,' Maung Maung Myint said. 'When people are poor they will blame each other.'

&#10052; ✿ ✿ ✿ ✿ ✿ &#10052;

Referring to Buddhism's 'three jewels', the nine attributes of the Buddha, the six attributes of his teachings, and the nine attributes of the *sangha*, 969 was cloaked in Buddhist respectability. The movement was personified by the same maroon-robed monks whose image had just a few years earlier been associated only with courage and righteousness. The irony was not lost on Maung Maung Myint, who during the Saffron Revolution of 2007 marched shoulder to shoulder with the monks, his clenched fist raised with theirs, feeling part of their cause, part of the nation. He was with the monks as they streamed past Shwedagon Pagoda, and up Inya Road to the American Embassy. He shouted the same slogans as them, demanding democracy as they advanced down University Avenue towards the house of Aung San Suu Kyi. He was there when Suu Kyi, still under house arrest, had come to her gate, her hands pressed together in obeisance, to show her solidarity. 'We were together then, and full of hope,' he said. 'Now I think, is this what we fought for? Democracy has not brought us freedom, it has not brought us anything.' Maung Maung Myint used to travel regularly to Upper Burma, to Pakokku and Arakan state, to buy pulses for export. 'Now I can't go upcountry,' he said. 'I don't know what would happened to me if I went there.'

In 2013, the black-slippered, red-robed monks were still marching. The news photographs looked identical to the pictures of the 2007 marches, when the monks called for freedom. This time, they were not protesting against army oppression; they were protesting against Muslims, seemingly against their very existence in Burma. New freedom of communication had allowed this movement to flourish; the Internet was their most powerful weapon. Extremist websites and posts on

Facebook had helped to whip up anti-Muslim sentiment. Wirathu's sermons were quickly posted online and distributed across the country on DVDs. In his quiet, mesmerising voice, the diminutive monk warned that Muslims could outbreed Buddhists, steal away Buddhist women and take over Burma's economy with injections of cash from sympathisers in the Arabian Gulf. 'But once these evil Muslims have control, they will not let us practise our religion. We must be careful. These Muslims really hate us,' Wirathu prophesised in a YouTube address. 'If you buy from Muslim shops, your money doesn't just stop there. It will eventually go towards destroying your race and religion.' Facebook messages in support of 969 were laden with patriotic sentiment. 'I love my country and I love my race!! #969,' read one post. Another Facebook page, 'Islam Virus', had attracted 11,875 'likes', posting slogans such as 'Oppose Islam: They breed like rabbits.' Even more sinister messages called for 'Kalar Beheading', while status updates purportedly posted by Muslims also sought to incite violence. 'Facebook is a problem,' said Maung Maung Myint. 'Some people write things under Muslim names. But in fact they are extremist Buddhists. Extremists stir this up. The people go out, they want their revenge on Muslims.'

⋆ ✿ ✿ ✿ ✿ ✿ ⋆

It was time for evening prayers in the Muslim dominated suburb of Mingalar Taung Nyunt, and the wooden cubbyholes outside the entrance to the mosque were filled with shoes. Young boys in white crocheted caps kicked off their flip-flops and hurried inside to the madrasa to join their classmates reciting the Koran in a collective, high-pitched drone. Headscarfed women sat at pavement stalls frying golden samosas for when the worshippers emerged. Cars growled up the street behind them, their progress slowed by potholes, food wagons and barely supervised children playing under the dim sodium lamps. The scene was just as it should have been at nightfall, and as it had been for decades. But if I had come to Mingalar Taung Nyunt just a week before, I would have found something very different.

For several months after the deadly riots in Meiktila, normal life in Mingalar Taung Nyunt came to a halt. Residents were frightened, and, having no faith that the police would protect them in the face of attack, went about organising their own defences. The road where I was standing had been closed to traffic, and each end shut off with makeshift corrugated tin barricades. Every side street and alleyway was guarded by a group of men, and at intervals along the street were stashed wooden clubs and iron bars, kept under lock to be used in the event of attack. The men of the neighbourhood had organised themselves into vigilante cells and, taking it in turns to sleep, would patrol until dawn. The familiar rhythm of life had disappeared, their businesses shunned, their children taunted at school. 'Go back to India! Go back to Bangladesh!' the son of one of the vigilantes was told. 'My son was totally confused. He always believed he was from Burma. I too have always considered myself as a Burmese.'

But as months passed without violence, the Muslims of Mingalar Taung Nyunt felt an easing of tension. Eventually, the community leaders decided to dismantle the barricades that divided them from the Buddhist quarters next door. The arms caches were removed, and I walked freely down the little side streets to peer into the living rooms which had always opened directly on to the street, where families ate and watched television, with little distinction between their private and public lives. At the corner teashop, where cigarette lighters hung down on strings for customers to light their cheroots, an old man with a grey stubble beard and milky blue eyes came and sat down next to me. The violence of the past year had not been spontaneous, he told me; hardliners in the military, perturbed by the pace of reform, were fomenting trouble, creating a pretext for the army to maintain power in Burma. In Sittwe, Meiktila and Lashio security forces had stood by while Muslims were killed, the elderly man said. In the lead-up to elections in 2015, sectarian relations would deteriorate, he predicted. The old man was born in Burma, as were his ancestors, for as far back as the family can remember. 'My great-great-grandfather was a soldier in the royal army of King Mindon,' he said. 'I have records, I can show you.' This man was born under Japanese occupation. His family had survived the war and avoided the mass expulsion of the 1960s. He had suffered discrimination all his life, he said, but had never experienced a time like this. 'This transition time is dangerous,' he told me. 'Some people are winners; some are not. They want someone to blame, and it is we Muslims. For us, this is the worst time we have known.'

✿ ✿ ✿ ✿ ✿

Back downtown, at the Bengali Sunni Jameh mosque, Maung Maung Myint's phone kept bleeping at his belt. Respected for his cool head and his sensible decision-making abilities, he had become a leader of the neighbourhood watch groups across the city, with activities coordinated by SMS. 'If anything happens I hear about it in a few minutes. Across the country, I know what is happening. Just fifteen minutes at the most and I will have a report.' Maung Maung Myint knows retaliation could spell disaster for Burma's Muslims. 'We supervise our community not to be violent,' he said, but acknowledged he was a dove among ever-proliferating hawks. He had lost weight in the last year and some of his instinctive good humour. The stress of moderation had taken its toll. But he would not hear talk of leaving Burma. 'This is where I was born,' he said. 'I am loyal to this land, and, *Inshallah,* this is where I will die.'

# 16
# Come Back Home

Things are better now, Mu Mu says, now she has a passport, a proper ID. No one can get her now. She's safe. She's got a good job, for an American lady, a single mother – well, almost a single mother: the daddy isn't around much, he's usually in Jakarta or some other city. There are two children and a very big dog; she was scared of the dog at first, but now she's used to it. Jenny pays her well, and she can cook now. She forgot to tell me that Jenny has taught her all sorts of recipes and she cooks the family meal every night. They all sit down together to eat. 'Can you imagine,' she says, 'Me as a cook?'

Mu Mu is back in Bangkok. I emailed her and she agreed to meet me on a Sunday evening as I passed through the city on my way home from Rangoon. We are sitting in my small hotel room, me on the edge of the bed, she on the chair. I offer her a drink – some tea, something from the minibar? She has anticipated that, and pulls out a small carton of juice from her bag, with a little straw attached. 'Don't worry, I've got my own,' she says. Mu Mu hates to be any trouble.

It's more than a year since she left the refugee camp. She is still carrying the extra weight she gained at the crisp factory: her short limbs look rounded and puffy, her once tiny waistline has thickened. She points all this out to me, of course. And she has aged. There are no creases or dark spots on her still beautiful, twenty-seven-year-old face, but a new hardness – eventually, the disappointment and injustice were bound to exact their toll.

✤ ✿ ✿ ✿ ✿ ✿ ✤

Mu Mu's friend Wan was one of the last to leave Mae La for America. The ritual of waving off the air-conditioned buses, as the chosen few headed for the glass-and-steel airport in Bangkok and onward to a new life, had lifted the spirits of those who remained behind. A few more left the camp for 'third countries' but after that there seemed to be a noticeable drop-off in activity by United Nations staff, and then they stopped coming altogether. The camp's residents were told nothing. Mu Mu's life continued as normal, drinking tea in the cool early morning, off to work at the potato chip shack, then back to wash her clothes in her plastic basin, dinner cooked over a charcoal burner, a gathering of friends in one of the huts. But, with no punctuation, the simple life began to lose its appeal. The realisation that there would be no happy ending to her story, not this time – no airline tickets, no visas, no warm jackets and proper shoes – descended on her slowly, silently, until it weighed on her so heavily she could no longer ignore it. The resettlement programme was ending. As the world saw it, things were getting better in Burma, while getting worse in plenty of other places. Around the globe there were new crises, new despots to worry about and new refugees whose needs were greater. The persecuted people of Burma had become last decade's cause.

Across the border from the camp, in Karen state, Mu Mu's homeland, the world's longest guerrilla struggle had come to a standstill. The Karen National Union, the insurgent army that had been fighting the Burmese government without pause since 1949, had agreed to cease fire. With dreams of creating its own mountain state with the mythical-sounding name of Kawthoolei, the KNU had held out through every truce agreed by the other ethnic groups over the decades, its demands unmet and compromise inconceivable. But, in 2011, there came a push by Burma's new civilian leaders to bring an end to the long and costly war, which had been the theatre of some of the most despicable atrocities – rape, child abductions and sadistic executions – of the modern age. An historic ceasefire agreement, signed in early 2012 in Mu Mu's hometown of Hpa'an, would help the Burmese government persuade foreign powers, such at the United States, to relax economic sanctions. President Thein Sein was starting to normalise relations with the Western nations that had once spurned Burma, and by November that year his reform efforts were given the highest endorsement – a visit by Barack Obama, the first serving US president to set foot in Burma.

Against this backdrop, officials met in Washington and Bangkok to discuss the long-running programme of resettling Burmese refugees overseas. Since 2005, the United States alone had taken more than 105,000 people, mostly ethnic Karen refugees from the camps along the Thai-Burma border, offering them citizenship and a new life in America. But now there were more pressing needs elsewhere, refugees from

Syria, Iraq and Congo. With the fighting paused, the Karen people who had fled across the border would have to start thinking of going home and, what's more, money for the camps would be cut. The United States and other donors had decided to spend more of their aid money inside Burma, as a way of encouraging and rewarding the political reforms.

Mu Mu didn't know this, she wasn't told and didn't have the means to find out, but it became clear to her nonetheless. By the time she had made the decision to leave Mae La, she had been told the only country still offering asylum to refugees from the camp was Russia. 'That was the only place,' she said. 'I don't know about Russia, all I know is that it is cold there, always snow, and also I have no friends there. That's when I decided to give up.'

❦ ✿ ✿ ✿ ✿ ✿ ❧

When Mu Mu and I lived in Bangkok, we shared the same neighbourhood, the same sunlight and polluted air, we used the same shops and tuk-tuks, but our experiences were completely different. My skin colour afforded me special, colonial-style privileges, I was a routine beneficiary of the Asian obsession with a fair complexion. Mu Mu had brown skin, a hill-tribe nose and an accent that marked her out as a migrant. She had walked into Thailand without a passport, and all she had was a 'pink card', a kind of amnesty document given to Burmese domestic workers at a price, allowing them to work in the homes of their employers.

One afternoon, when walking down our *soi*, off the busy shopping thoroughfare of Thong Lor, Mu Mu was arrested. I thought I knew the two policemen who did it – they were friendly enough, in their brown, belted uniforms; they would melt with delight when I strolled past pushing my blond-haired, blue-eyed daughter. They would lean down to pinch the chubby folds of her arms, like a couple of doting grandmothers. *Narak! Narak!* – So cute! – they would say, seemingly thrilled each time we passed by. They were not so friendly to Mu Mu. The hot sun directly overhead, she stepped in front of them carrying her small wallet and a plastic bag of supermarket shopping. They called out for her to stop. They were serious, unsmiling. She put the bag down between her feet. They demanded to see her ID, and she retrieved the dog-eared pink card. It was a noisy, busy intersection, motorcycle taxi drivers in orange vests leaned into the corner just inches from her back. There was a wedding dress shop behind them and a street stall selling grilled fish and som-tam to their left. Pedestrians rushed past, heads down, keen to get to the shade of the fig trees beyond. If they had looked, they would have seen the officers passing the pink piece of paper between them, one of them jabbing his finger at it, questioning the girl. Then they would have seen Mu Mu, in a pink T-shirt, pedal-pusher jeans and little plastic-heeled sandals, climb behind an officer on to one of the police motorbikes, her head down, clutching the bag of shopping on her lap.

At home with my daughter, starting to wonder what had delayed Mu Mu, I received a phone call from her friend Mie. Mu Mu was in Thong Lor police station, they had found something wrong with her pink card, Mie and her husband would go and sort it out, they would take money. I heard nothing more for three hours. Mu Mu's phone was switched off, Mie wasn't answering. Then, just as it was getting dark, I heard the gate to our front yard squeak and Mu Mu's kitten heels clicking on the concrete. She came in, sat down on the living room floor, apologised for causing trouble and began to cry. My daughter climbed into her lap. 'Did they hurt you? Did they touch you?' I asked. No, she said, but she was scared. They told her there was an error on her pink card (it was written in Thai, which neither she nor I could read), she would have to pay money. 'They shouted at me,' Mu Mu said. 'They called me some bad things.' The negotiation was led by Mie's husband, and they ended up paying 2,000 baht, more than $50, to get Mu Mu out. It was a reminder of how vulnerable she was. In Bangkok, Mu Mu occupied two very different spaces. In our safe, domestic haven we liked to think of her as one of the family. But out on the streets, Mu Mu was just another illegal migrant.

❧ ✿ ✿ ✿ ✿ ✿ ❧

So, Mu Mu has a passport now. It's not a full passport, but it allows her to move freely between Burma and Thailand. The passports are a new thing, an acknowledgement of the massive amount of human traffic across the border, an attempt to regularise it. Mu Mu can now move around legally in Thailand; no more trekking over mountain passes, no more hiding under tarpaulins in the backs of trucks, and a simple trip to the supermarket no longer holds fear. On a practical level, things are good for her: she has a secure job, she is valued by her employer, she is paid well. She can buy things for herself, new clothes, a nice handbag and books. Mu Mu loves reading, she enjoys history, military history especially, she says. But her favourite books are of the motivational, self-help genre; she has become quite addicted to them. A little bashfully, she pulls one out of her bag to show me, with the title *The Successful You.* 'I don't know why,' she says, 'I just can't stop reading these ones.'

But as straightforward as her life seems now, leaving the camp, letting go of the dream of America, had been another disappointment, another small death inside her. 'My dream is broken,' she says. 'I'm still waiting for my life to start.' At her insistence, her parents have sold their house in Hpa'an, have paid off their creditors as best they can, and are living, working, scraping by in the small town of Myawaddy on the Thai border. Migrant workers often keep going with the thought of the house they will build back home, the bricks and mortar that will be the dividend of their hard work and their security in the future. Mu Mu has absolutely nothing to show for her years of toil. She used to be someone who loved to be surrounded by friends and laughter. Now she guards the time she has alone. She likes to sit in her room at Jenny's house, and think about her ex-boyfriend Saw Myo and the happy times they spent together, when they were in love. Those memories are her only valued possession. 'When I am alone, I can miss him,' she says.

❧ ✿ ✿ ✿ ✿ ✿ ✤

In Burma, change was continuing apace. When I met up again with Mu Mu in late 2013, the government had just awarded licences to two foreign telecommunications companies, from Norway and Qatar, to operate mobile phone networks across the country. I may have seen many more people chatting on their cell phones in bustling Rangoon, but in digital technology Burma still stood out only for being at the bottom of the rankings, a position it held on so many measures. Less than 10 per cent of its fifty million people were connected by cell phone, one of the lowest rates of mobile usage anywhere in the world. That would change in the coming years: the mobile phone, that symbol of freedom and independence that Mu Mu treasured so dearly, would become affordably available to millions more Burmese – from the mountains of Chin state to the mangrove swamps of the Irrawaddy

Delta. More and more Burmese would be connected not just to each other, but to the outside world, with 3G technology and smartphones giving access to global information networks for the first time. The lifting of Burma's pariah status in the international arena had brought an opening of its physical connections too: airlines that had excluded military-ruled Burma from their flight schedules added new routes to Rangoon, linking the city for the first time to Qatar, Frankfurt, Hong Kong and Tokyo.

Reforms in the financial sector, seemingly far removed from the lives of ordinary Burmese, had the potential to make a significant impact. For decades the Burmese currency, the kyat, was fixed at an official rate at least a hundred times higher than its value on the black market. The system not only confused and perplexed foreign investors, it also allowed Burma's military rulers to expropriate billions of dollars of revenue from state-owned enterprises, siphoning money into foreign bank accounts that actually belonged in the national budget. But in 2012, the currency was set at a market-based rate, its value against the US dollar determined each day by a foreign exchange auction in Naypyidaw. Now there was effectively just one rate, whether you were exchanging dollars for kyat on a Rangoon street or in a state-run bank. But why would that matter to the millions of rural poor, the majority of Burma's citizens, who had never held a dollar bill in their lives?

The reason was this: in the past, more than 40 per cent of budgeted revenues, from taxes or royalties from exports of gas and other raw materials, went 'off budget', according to an economist working at a Western embassy in Rangoon. The money was converted to kyats at the false, official rate, allowing chunks of the country's wealth to be salted away into the private offshore bank accounts of the generals. This stole funds from the already meagre provision that the military government set aside for spending on health and education – estimated at best at 2.5 per cent of national income in each sector. The new economic reforms promised a bigger share of the budget earmarked for these sectors, albeit from a pitifully low base, while an end to the dual exchange rate would bolster the pot of funds from which that spending could be drawn. In short, this could mean more of the income from Burma's abundant natural resources finally benefitting its impoverished people in the form of vaccination programmes, new health clinics, trained teachers and better-equipped schools.

On the Chinese border, in the town of Laiza, in the northern state of Kachin, Burma's armed ethnic groups met in early November 2013 to discuss a national ceasefire accord. Some of those at the meeting compared it to the Panglong conference of 1947, the famous gathering in the Shan hills of ethnic leaders and General Aung San that led to an accord that was never implemented, a prelude to more than six decades of civil war. While a ceasefire was in place in Karen state, another truce, in the highlands of Kachin, had collapsed in 2011, reigniting a conflict between government soldiers and Kachin Independence Army rebels. The fighting had uprooted more than a hundred thousand civilians from their homes, scattering them into dirty, crowded displacement camps, exposed to freezing winter temperatures. Just days before the talks, Burmese media reported attacks by Tatmadaw troops on Kachin villages. Nevertheless, the Laiza conference, a precursor to talks with government negotiators, was seen as a first step towards cementing ceasefires in all ethnic areas, raising the prospect of guns falling silent across Burma for the first time since independence.

✿ ✿ ✿ ✿ ✿

Mu Mu looks tired. Talking about her life, and listening too, is draining. We allow ourselves to be distracted by something on CNN. I turn up the volume and we watch, amused, as a daredevil walks a tightrope across the Grand Canyon. We share some cashew nuts from the minibar. When the item finishes, I turn the TV down again and ask her warily about the future. I expect she has run out of dreams by now. But Mu Mu surprises me.

Mu Mu knows about the changes back in Burma. She knows about the ceasefire, she knows that fighting has stopped, for now at least, in the Karen hills. But most importantly to her, she knows that Burma is no longer run by men in uniform. She wants to see the positive. 'They say it is changing. I am happy that there are no soldiers in government. All my life there have been soldiers. We want to have a change.' For Mu Mu, political reform in Burma is not an abstract concept. It is something that is happening to her. 'We felt unlucky that we had to leave our country. We always wondered why it was like that for us. Now I can go back and live in my town, like other people do, live in the town where they were born.'

I look up from scribbling her words in my notebook. I'm amazed. Did she really just say that? Mu Mu continues, her voice strong; she is making a speech, a statement of intent. She may not know it, but her words echo Aung San Suu Kyi's rallying cries for a collective effort. 'Now I can go back to my country,' Mu Mu says. 'I want to do something good in my life. I want to join in. We need to change our way of thinking, not just think about ourselves. If we care about each other our country can go up. This is our opportunity.'

Later, in darkness, I walk Mu Mu down the street to the skytrain station. We pass a glass-fronted foot massage parlour – the customers in candlelit semi-slumber, their lower legs wrapped in towels, as strong fingers ease the aches and knots of weary city limbs – this is a typical Bangkok neighbourhood. We head down Sukhumvit Soi 53 and past, coincidentally, the very spot where Mu Mu was disgorged from a pickup truck thirteen years earlier, an adolescent migrant who had already discounted the possibility of a future in her homeland. We turn into the echoing cacophony of Sukhumvit Road, beneath the elevated concrete of the skytrain station. In front of the neon-lit 7-Eleven, we hug goodbye. From the pavement, I watch as the escalator carries Mu Mu smoothly up to the platform. Walking back, in the warm night, I consider what she has told me. Although Burma's opening had often been described as a transformation from the top, real change, I think, can only come from the bottom, from people like Mu Mu, through their commitment and courage. The people of Burma are responsible for their own future, and a peaceful transition can only come if voices like Mu Mu's can drown out the clamour of suspicion and discord. 'We have been unhappy too long,' she had told me. 'Now it is in our hands. We people need to make the change.'

# Afterword

Win Tin, the brave and principled journalist, politician and former prisoner, died of kidney failure in Rangoon General Hospital on 21 April 2014, aged eighty-four, just before this book went to print.

Radical, irrepressible and mischievous to the last, he asked visitors to his hospital bed to sneak in paper and pens – against the express orders of his doctors – so that he could continue to write his political articles, poems and letters.

Following his release from Insein Prison in September 2008, Win Tin's home had been a little two-roomed cabin given to him by his close friend Ohn Tun. There his only valued possessions, his books, were stacked high on shelves above his writing desk. He owned a narrow bed, and one luxury: a television with a satellite link-up that allowed him to watch Champions League football.

Life had become more comfortable, but Win Tin never saw himself as free. To his dying day he wore blue – the colour of his prison uniform – in a show of solidarity with Burma's thousands of other political prisoners. 'While there are others still in prison, we are not free,' he had told me. 'Burma is one big, open-air prison.' After 2011, under the presidency of Thein Sein, most of Burma's prisoners of conscience were released. But by the time of Win Tin's death, more than thirty still remained behind bars, including fellow journalist Zaw Phay, and Win Tin never saw a justification to change the colour of his clothes.

There was no gentle decline for Win Tin, no reflective autumn years for him. From the moment he left jail he was working again, delighted to be still alive and able to continue his life's mission: to expel the military from Burmese political life. After his death, I listened to the recordings I had made of our interviews, to the careful accounts he gave of his life, in his croaky, eager voice. 'When I was in prison I worried that I might not be very useful when I came out, I thought I would be senile. But then I realised I had to take part,' he had told me at our first meeting at the top of Sakura Tower. 'So from the very first minute I got out of the car that brought me from jail, I had to start to give my opinions. I decided I should express myself honestly and clearly.'

Win Tin lived to see the release from house arrest of Aung San Suu Kyi, and on their reunion had to wipe away tears, a rare display of emotion from a man who had endured so much. He witnessed the beginnings of a reform process under President Thein Sein, the first steps, perhaps, towards Win Tin's vision of a democratic future for Burma. It was more progress than many had dared hope for, but was certainly not enough for Win Tin. He remained at the radical end of the NLD, and regarded his party's relationship with the president as far too conciliatory. Win Tin always spoke truth to power; he had no compunction about questioning the political tactics of his leader Suu Kyi. He voiced reservations about her decision to enter parliament – joining, as he saw it, a corrupt political system based on an illegitimate constitution. But as a friend and confidant, he was steadfastly loyal.

For the younger generation of democracy activists, many of them born when he was in jail, Win Tin was an inspiration. In the overflowing chaos of the NLD's offices, he would listen to them, gently advise them, lend them books and papers. He was also keen to learn from them, fascinated by technology and new ways to communicate his party's message. 'Now we are determined to work harder to achieve democracy,' NLD youth member Khin Lay told the news channel DVB after Win Tin's death. 'It was something he never got the chance to see.'

On the day of Win Tin's funeral in Rangoon, I was shocked to see on my Facebook feed a photograph of him lying in a glass-topped coffin. It was difficult image to look at, but also comforting to see the love and care with which he had been prepared for burial. Win Tin lay on a bed of hundreds of jasmine flowers, wearing a crisply pressed blue shirt, *longyi* and his trademark black-rimmed glasses. The mourners, of course, wore blue.

'Win Tin was a truly an honest man. He courageously stood against injustice. He never gave up or allowed those who incarcerated him to be victorious,' the poet and songwriter Ko Ye Lwin said at his graveside. 'He was the undefeated.'

# Acknowledgements

Above all, my sincere thanks go to all the people who trusted me to tell their stories in this book, for their bravery in talking openly in a country where half a century of repressive rule has left a legacy of fear and suspicion.

I'm very grateful to Myint Kyaw, Eaint Khaine Oo, Zayar Hlaing, Han Thar and Aung Kyaw Myint who all helped to arrange and translate interviews for me and gave me invaluable guidance and friendship during my years in Burma.

In Rangoon I'd also like to thank Gabrielle Paluch, Sann Oo, Hay Soe, Honey Cho, Susanne Kempel, Daniel Gelfer, Thant Myint-U, Bron and Tamas Wells, Thiha Maung Maung, Ruth Bradley-Jones, Maung Maung Lwin, Andrew Kirkwood and Kelly Macdonald.

Some of the material in this book comes from my reporting for the *Independent*, where Andy Buncombe and Archie Bland were fantastically supportive.

Andrew Gray, Martin Smith, Peter Popham, Ben Rogers, Helen Bendon, Sean Turnell, Thin Lei Win, Katie Nguyen, Lin Noueihed and Daniel Simpson all gave great advice and encouragement along the way.

Thank you to Celia Russell, Adam Manolson and Chanm Nyein Zaw for carefully reading the manuscript and spotting my many mistakes. Many thanks also to Anthony Spratt for drawing a beautiful map.

I am extremely grateful to Andrew Lownie for his faith in my book and tireless support. Thanks to my brilliant editors Emily Sweet and Justine Taylor, and Narisa Chakrabongse and everyone at River Books.

Finally, special thanks to the Russell and Collison families, especially Dan, Ruby and Mattie Collison.